Experts Rave About TYPE & LAYOUT

A surprising and useful book, full of information and indispensable to anyone involved in communicating ideas through typographic means.
— Milton Glaser, Graphic Designer, President,
    Milton Glaser, Inc.

All of us who are prepared to take the offensive in the crusade for the future of print have been handed a tool of great value in this lively book by Colin Wheildon. For designers, editors, ad makers, and publishers who would like their work to work.
    — John Mack Carter, Editor-in-Chief and Director
        of Magazine Development, Hearst Magazines

Now there's nothing left to argue about! At last conjecture, tradition and hearsay have been replaced by the irrefutable logic of numbers and scientific survey results. *Now when you break the rules, you can predict how many reader's you'll lose!*
    — Roger C. Parker, Author, *Looking Good in Print,*
        The One-Minute Designer and *Desktop Publishing and*
        Design for Dummies

"If you want good contact with [readers] and want them to understand the content of your message you should listen to Wheildon.... A very rewarding discussion, one that is thoughtful and packed with proved information."
    — *Communication Arts*

Bravissimo! *Type & Layout* may well be the most important book on print design and typography ever published. In the words of Vrest Orton, founder of The Vermont Country Store:

"If you pick up a book or a magazine and exclaim, 'Oh, isn't this beautiful type!' the designer has failed. Any type that gets in between the reader and the author is not doing its job."

Colin Wheildon has thoroughly researched the art and science of effective print communications and has managed to turn complex ideas and issues into exquisitely understandable and readable English.

Every publisher, advertiser, writer, and designer *must* own this modern masterpiece! It is to design and typography what William Strunk, Jr. and E.B. White's *Elements of Style* is to prose.

—Denison Hatch, Editor, *Target Marketing*
and *Who's Mailing What!*

"The trouble with my students, " said the Harvard professor, "isn't just that they don't know anything. They don't even *suspect* anything."

Colin Wheildon suspects *everything*–and he has unearthed knowledge that can give a dollars-in-your-pocket advantage to any art director or designer with the wit to take it to heart.

—Joel Raphaelson, former Executive Creative Director, Ogilvy & Mather Chicago; co-author, *Writing That Works*, and editor, *The Unpublished David Ogilvy*

It's reassuring to find that the typographic truths I have preached for years have some basis in hard evidence. Typography is getting increasingly chaotic. Some of it is ugly, much of it is unreadable. But I think the intent, in most cases, is to attract readers.

If Wheildon's data convinces designers of a more rational typography in order to achieve comprehension, it may have the unintended effect of making type more beautiful in the bargain. That would be welcome.

—Tom Suzuki, Graphic Designer, Tom Suzuki, Inc.

This book is a must-read for any editor and designer involved with newsletters. It gives reader-oriented editors ammunition when fighting for readability with designers and solves ongoing debates such as: *How dark a screen is too dark? Where do we place spot color? Should text be justified or ragged right?* And it does so with results from conscientious research (not samples of 10!).

In an effort to dress up what often feels like "the same old layout," newsletter designers break many of the rules in this book, including placing headlines in the middle of articles, using screened artwork behind text, reversing type, and setting body copy in sans serif type. The comprehension statistics presented in *Type & Layout* should make any designer stop and think carefully before breaking any of the rules.

—Elaine Floyd, Author, *Marketing with Newsletters* and *Advertising from the Desktop*

This book has been long needed. Now we finally have the definitive guidelines that will make advertising far more effective and can save millions of dollars now wasted by poor advertising typography.

Colin Wheildon has done an excellent job. He has blended solid research with the common sense that has marked his distinguished career. And he has a writing style that makes this a pleasure to read.

Don't be put off by the fact that he is practicing in Australia. He demonstrates convincingly that the intricate process of reading is shared by every human who has two eyes and one brain—north or south of the equator makes no difference.

—Edmund C. Arnold, Columnist and Consultant to
    Publications

Hitherto designers have had to rely on their guesses as to what works best in choosing the typography and layout. All too often they guess wrong. Thanks to Colin Wheildon, they no longer have to guess. No guesswork here. *Only facts.*

—From the Foreword by David Ogilvy

One can probably learn more from this single book about how typography and layout communicate than one would from several years of study at design school.

—Heikki Ratalahti, Graphics Designer, Jayme, Ratalahti,
    Inc.

Wheildon's research—and this book—are an excellent antidote to desktop typesetting's license to kill communications.
—Paul Swift, Managing Editor, *The Newsletter on Newsletters*

For the first time, I know *why* and *what* makes me read, understand, and act when I read an ad. It is magic.
—Martin P. Levin, Counsel, Cowan, Leibowitz & Latman; formerly President, Times-Mirror Book Company and Chairman, American Association of Publishers

With so many typefaces and so little knowledge, college students should be considered armed and dangerous. *Type & Layout* should be required reading before students are allowed to touch a computer.
—Dennis G. Martin, Ph.D., Professor of Communications, Brigham Young University

Next time an art director hell-bent on "creativity" runs your headline sideways in all caps and sets your body in white on black sans serif, fire the hotshot, and as a parting gift present him or her with Colin Wheildon's masterful book, which reveals everything the true professional needs to know about using type, design, and originality—not to grandstand but to truly communicate.
—Bill Jayme, Copywriter, Jayme, Ratalahti, Inc.

STOP! Before you design your next printed piece or approve a design submitted for your approval, be sure to read every word of Colin Wheildon's great new book, *Type & Layout*. The material it contains is so vital it can more than double the comprehension of your message.

I've been teaching courses on newspaper, magazine, direct mail, and catalog design for nearly 50 years. Unfortunately, many of the "rules" of effective design and typography I've offered have been based primarily on age-old truisms or minor research studies.

But Colin Wheildon has changed all that. For the first time there is a body of statistically significant research to show which techniques achieve the objective of all printed material: maximum communication with readers.

What Colin Wheildon has to say is particularly important in this age of desktop publishing where "amateurs" often are asked to make decisions concerning design and typography. Nobody should be allowed to sit down at a computer to create anything for reproduction until they have completely reviewed the results of this landmark research.

The information Colin Wheildon provides is far from just more theory. I discovered his research a few years ago and had an opportunity to discuss it with him. I then convinced some of my clients to conduct tests to verify his findings in the marketplace. They quickly discovered better comprehension led to increased sales!

—Dick Hodgson, President, Sargeant House

This is a book that everyone in advertising should have by their side. Apple should include a copy of it with every Macintosh sold. There's lots of room for improving layout and the use of type, and Colin Wheildon explains how to do it.

—Charles A. Mouser, Advertising Consultant,
President, Mouser Institute of Advertising

This book is much needed by students and professionals alike. Colin Wheildon substantiates what many have long felt intuitively: that there are human factors explaining why certain type and layout approaches work better than others. The correlation between the creative and business sides of print communications explored in this book should be considered by anyone concerned about the cost-effectiveness of a publication or advertisement.

–Tony Crouch, Director, Design and Production,
University of California Press

Here is earthshaking research which could significantly increase the effectiveness of every dollar every advertiser spends in newspapers. If readers act on the facts Colin reveals in this book, "wealth beyond the dreams of avarice" could be theirs. If not, well, everyone's got the right to go to hell their own way. So read and remember: belief without action is worthless!

—Reg Mowat, Founding Executive Director, Newspaper
Advertising Bureau of Australia, formerly Director,
Foote Cone & Belding Australia

"Open Your Eyes and Listen" is the title of a seminar on type I've been giving for years. Type is speech made visible, with all the nuances, inflections, tonalities, and even dialects of the human voice. What a marvelous medium! It is one of humanity's most precious possessions—so hoorah for *Type and Layout* in crystallizing good practice in trustworthy, dependable proof. Now we can all point to chapter-and-verse. Immensely useful.

 –Jan White, Communication Design Consultant and
  Author, *Editing by Design*

Wheildon's book is refreshingly realistic—focusing on the way type *works* instead of just the way it looks. It scientifically proves some long-held assumptions and makes other surprising and important discoveries.

 At a time when many designers and clients think that a good design is "something that wins awards," this book demonstrates in no uncertain terms that the point of all these little marks on paper is to send a comprehensible message to the reader. It clearly proves that many current design trends unwisely trade effectiveness for fashion. *Anyone who wants to get the most out of words on their page will want this book.*

 —Daniel Will-Harris, Designer and Author of *TypeStyle:*
  how to choose and use type on a personal computer

All I can say about this book is that from this moment on, I will never work with a layout artist who has not read it!

 —Jerry Huntsinger, Direct Mail Fundraising Copywriter,
  Author, and Columnist

Type & Layout

Type & Layout

How typography and design can
get your message across—or get in the way

Colin Wheildon

Foreword by David Ogilvy

Edited and with an Introduction by Mal Warwick

Afterword by Tony Antin

STRATHMOOR
PRESS

Berkeley, California

Printed in Canada.   ISBN 0-9624891-5-8

Published March 1995 by Strathmoor Press, Inc. Second printing January 1997. For more information, contact: Strathmoor Press, Inc., 2550 Ninth Street, Suite 1040, Berkeley, California 94710-2516, phone (510) 843-8888, e-mail info@strathmoor.com

Library of Congress Cataloging-in-Publication Data
Wheildon, Colin, 1936–
        Type & layout: how typography and design can get your message across, or get in the way / Colin Wheildon; foreword by David Ogilvy; edited and with an introduction by Mal Warwick; afterword by Tony Antin.
        p.   cm.
        Includes bibliographical references and index.
        ISBN 0-9624891-5-8 (pbk.)
        1. Printing, Practical-Layout.   2. Graphic Arts.   I. Warwick, Mal.
II. Title: III. Title: Type and Layout.
        Z246.W53 1995
        686.2'2-dc20   94-48089

9 8 7 6 5 4 3 2

§

Contents

§

Foreword

THIS BOOK MARKS A MILESTONE.

If you write advertisements for a living, as I do, it is a matter of life and death that what you write should be read by potential customers. It's the headline and copy that do the selling.

The tragedy is that the average advertisement is read by only four per cent of people on their way through the publication it appears in. Most of the time, this is the fault of the so-called "art director" who designs advertisements. If he is an aesthete at heart—and most of them are—he doesn't care a damn whether anybody *reads* the words. He regards them as mere elements in his pretty design. In many cases he blows away half the readers by choosing the wrong type. But he doesn't care. He should be boiled in oil.

Fortunately, there are some art directors who do care. They do their best to design advertisements in such a way as to maximize reading. But hitherto, in making decisions about the typography and layout, they have had to rely on their guesses as to what works best. All too often they guess wrong. Thanks to Colin Wheildon, they no longer have to guess.

Some ways work better. This book reveals what they are.

No guesswork here. *Only facts.*

Not long ago, I read a magazine which carried 47 advertisements set in "reverse" (white copy set on a black background). These ads could not sell, because research has found that nobody *reads* white copy on a black background.

There are many other ways for art directors to *wreck* advertisements—or, for that matter, magazine or newspaper stories, annual reports, brochures, or any other sort of printed matter. This book reveals them all.

–David Ogilvy
Poitou, France, September 1994

§

What This Book
Can Do for You

WHY SHOULD ONE MAGAZINE advertisement gen-
erate thousands of inquiries—while a similar ad in the same
issue for a competing product falls flat?

How can one sales letter yield $1 million more in
revenue than a similar letter, mailed at the same time to a
statistically identical group of prospects?

And if a newspaper editorial on a City Hall scandal sets
off a public furor, why should a similar opinion piece go
largely ignored?

Depending on your trade, you might explain these differences in results in a great variety of ways. For example:

» An advertising executive may compare how well each message reflects deep understanding of its readers.

» The editor might ask how well thoughts are organized and how clearly they're expressed.

» A direct marketer is likely to look first at what the message offers readers.

» The designer may be most concerned with how the visual presentation strengthens (or hinders) the argument.

» A printer might examine the paper, the ink, and the quality of impression.

All these factors—and many more besides—can distinguish *effective* printed communications from those that fail to deliver the message. Often, there's no single "best" explanation. No communications specialist has all the answers.

This extraordinary little book explains how one factor in printed communications—typography—plays a role that specialists in other fields may find surprisingly large.

You'll benefit from this book whatever part you play in the long daisy chain from the creation of a printed message to its delivery into the hands of readers.

Figure 1

Does this ad represent "good" typographic design?

Colin Wheildon will teach you a thing or two whether you work in direct marketing, fundraising, design, editing, or typography—or if you're a student (or teacher) in any of those fields.

And that goes double if, like me, you're one of the millions just now discovering typefaces through the magic of desktop publishing. With so much sheer typographical power at our fingertips, we have the capacity to create written materials that reach new heights of unreadability.

Consider, for example, the magazine ad reproduced on the preceding page (Figure 1). It's eye-catching, and the type is elegant.

The advertisement in Figure 1, which appeared in a weekly newsmagazine, conveys an upscale image consistent with its sponsor's. To most of us, it looks like "good" typographic design.

But read this book, and you may gain a different opinion. In fact, there are five ways the ad in Figure 1 falls short as an effort to communicate:

» The headline appears in white, "reversed out" against a dark (blue) background.

» The headline is set all in capital letters.

» Even worse, the text of the ad is set in capitals, too.

» The headline copy ends in a period.

» The text is set ragged right rather than justified.

Colin Wheildon's research *proves* that each of these five aspects of Figure 1 undermines comprehension—and thus retention—in those who read it.

In this skeptical era, it takes a lot of nerve to claim a book can *prove* anything at all.

That's why this book is unique.

The worlds of printing, design, editing, and advertising abound with experts who have *opinions* about typography. As a magazine editor for 30 years and a typographer of long standing, Colin Wheildon has opinions of his own—but you'll have to write him a letter or call Australia to find out Wheildon's preferences in type. This book reports the results of nine years of his hard-nosed, rigorous *research*. The project involved repeated testing of more than 200 adults, using methodology recommended by academic researchers. You'll find Wheildon's discussion of the research program and the methodology he employed in Appendix 1.

THAT QUANTITATIVE CERTAINTY in Wheildon's research first attracted me six years ago to *Type & Layout*. A Canadian colleague, Harvey McKinnon—like me, a specialist in raising money by mail—passed along a copy of the study, a booklet entitled *Communicating–Or Just Making Pretty Shapes?* Harvey was impressed with Wheildon's matter-of-fact examination of the effects of typographic changes on the people who matter most: readers. After all, Harvey and I are both direct marketers. We *measure* the effects of everything we do (or at least we ought to!). Our work rises or falls on the strength of *results*.

Colin Wheildon showed us how to improve our results by making informed decisions about typography and design.

I've put his findings to work in my own mailings and print ads, urged them on clients and colleagues, and cited them in my seminars, articles, and books. I continue to do so, because Colin Wheildon's findings help me raise more money.

But the book you hold in your hands is different from the slender booklet Harvey McKinnon shared with me six years ago. There was a third edition published in Australia in 1990 (bringing the total in print there to 20,000 copies—a huge number for such a small population). In publishing this first book-length edition, I've made a number of significant additions:

» 62 illustrations drawn from U.S. publications—twice as many as appeared in the original.

» new material the author included in the third Australian edition.

» two new chapters, "Eight Ways to Ruin a Perfectly Good Ad" and "Six Sure-Fire Devices to Drive Away Your Readers," which I wrote with the author's consent.

» a glossary, which the author graciously consented to prepare expressly for this edition. You'll find there his straightforward definitions of the typographic terms in this book that may be unfamiliar to readers without a grounding in that specialty.

» an appendix about the methodology, "The Research Program," which is based on brief references in the Australian edition and correspondence with the author.

»   an index and guides to the statistical tables and illustrations, to enhance the book's value as a reference tool.

I've also made minor editorial changes, mostly to reflect common North American idiom and spelling rather than the Australian. However, there are no substantive differences between this book and its predecessors. All the changes I've introduced are part of an effort to make this book more *useful* to readers in the United States and Canada.

R EADERS WHO ARE INCLINED to be persnickety might argue that differences in the effectiveness of printed communications are mostly a matter of talent, training, and experience. Up to a point, they'd be right. Some editors are skilled wordsmiths, some designers brilliant image-makers, some marketers inspired—and some shouldn't be allowed within ten yards of a word-processor or desktop publishing system.

This book won't change that. Most of us, however, are at least minimally competent at our craft, whatever it may be. Otherwise, people wouldn't be likely to pay for the stuff we put out.

This book is for us. Genius or hack, student or teacher, those of us who seek to *communicate* through print can put Colin Wheildon's findings to work.

Try it! You'll see how easy it is.

And here's what else you'll see:

» More people will actually *read* the things you put into print.

» They'll *understand* better what you're trying to say.

» They'll *remember* more of your stuff.

But that's only the beginning. There's more:

» If you're selling things through print, people will probably buy more of them.

» If you're trying to persuade people, they'll be more likely to agree.

» If you're selling goods or raising money by mail, your revenue will increase.

Who knows what might happen? Why settle for petty dreams?

But first things first.

Read this book.

It will change forever the way you look at the printed page.

—Mal Warwick

§

Acknowledgments

I AM GRATEFUL FOR and honored by the continued support and encouragement given to me by my mentor and friend, Ed Arnold; by Tony Antin, a worthy ally in the fight against bad typography; by David Ogilvy, of Poitou, France, whose questioning, always positive and valid, was a constant source of stimulation; and by my publisher, Mal Warwick, whose expertise, advice, and unbounded enthusiasm have made this publication a reality.

To my wife, Lynn, who has lived with my research so closely she can recite the text from memory, and whose unswerving support and skills have been immeasurable, I gratefully dedicate this book.

ONE

Why This Study Matters

TYPOGRAPHY IS THE ART of designing a communication by using the printed word. It is employed in making newspapers, magazines, books, handbills, posters, greeting and business cards, pamphlets, and brochures . . . anything that is meant to be read.

Typography must be clear. At its best it is virtually invisible! It must also follow logic, the linearity of the alphabet, and the physiology of reading.

It is not the purpose of this study to provide enlightenment and great wisdom on graphic art. Nor is it my intention to say what is right and what is wrong with advertising, newspaper, magazine, or commercial typography.

Rather, my intention is to warn of the horrible damage some typographical elements, if used in the wrong context or thoughtlessly, can do to our creations. To put it bluntly, it's possible to blow away more than half our readers simply by choosing the wrong type.

Let's set the scene by having a look at Figure 2, a very simple design (see opposite page). We'll assume this layout occupies a page in a mass circulation newspaper or magazine, and that its eye-catching illustration and thought-provoking headline have attracted the attention of one million readers.

Figure 2

The Headline Goes Here, Under a Graphic

The text then starts here and continues without interruption in this three-column layout. Text is fully justified. This layout is the sort called Ayer No. 1. It is much favored in advertising circles. It is also found in magazines and newspapers—although most layout artists frown on such obvious simplicity. The text then starts here and continues without interruption in this three-column layout. Text is fully justified. This layout is the sort called Ayer No. 1. It is much favored in advertising circles. It is also found in magazines and newspapers—although most layout artists frown on such obvious simplicity. The text then starts here and continues without interruption in this three-column layout. Text is fully justified. This layout is the sort called Ayer No. 1. It is much favored in advertising circles. It is also found in magazines and newspapers—although most layout artists frown on such obvious simplicity. The text then starts here and continues without interruption in this three-column layout. Text is fully justified. This layout is the sort called Ayer No. 1. It is much favored in advertising circles. It is also found in magazines and newspapers—although most layout artists

frown on such obvious simplicity. The text then starts here and continues without interruption in this three-column layout. Text is fully justified. This layout is the sort called Ayer No. 1. It is much favored in advertising circles. It is also found in magazines and newspapers—although most layout artists frown on such obvious simplicity. The text then starts here and continues without interruption in this three-column layout. Text is fully justified. This layout is the sort called Ayer No. 1. It is much favored in advertising circles. It is also found in magazines and newspapers—although most layout artists frown on such obvious simplicity. The text then starts here and continues without interruption in this three-column layout. Text is fully justified. This layout is the sort called Ayer No. 1. It is much favored in advertising circles. It is also found in magazines and newspapers—although most layout artists frown on such obvious simplicity. The text then starts here and continues without interruption in this three-column layout. Text is fully justified. This layout is the sort called Ayer No. 1. It is much favored in advertising circles. It is also found in magazines and

newspapers—although most layout artists frown on such obvious simplicity. The text then starts here and continues without interruption in this three-column layout. Text is fully justified. This layout is the sort called Ayer No. 1. It is much favored in advertising circles. It is also found in magazines and newspapers—although most layout artists frown on such obvious simplicity. The text then starts here and continues without interruption in this three-column layout. Text is fully justified. This layout is the sort called Ayer No. 1. It is much favored in advertising circles. It is also found in magazines and newspapers—although most layout artists frown on such obvious simplicity. The text then starts here and continues without interruption in this three-column layout. Text is fully justified. This layout is the sort called Ayer No. 1. It is much favored in advertising circles. It is also found in magazines and newspapers—although most layout artists frown on such obvious simplicity. The text then starts here and continues without interruption in this three-column layout. Text is fully justified. This layout is the sort called Ayer No. 1. It is much favored in advertising circles. It is

A simple layout that helps the reader.

We've set the body matter in an elegant serif face, say, Garamond. Figure 3 (below) shows what this type looks like. Based on our research study, the chances are good that the message will be comprehended thoroughly by about 670,000, or slightly more than two-thirds, of the one million readers of our hypothetical newspaper or magazine who have been attracted by the article.

Figure 3

Assume we set the body matter in the layout on the preceding page (Figure 2) in this elegant serif face, ITC Garamond. The chances are good that the message will be comprehended thoroughly by about 670,000, or slightly more than two-thirds, of our readers.

A sample of ITC Garamond, an elegant serif face.

Now let's suppose we reset the type in a sans serif face, say Helvetica, reputedly one of the more legible sans serif faces. Figure 4 (below) shows how this looks. The chances now are that the message will be comprehended thoroughly by only 120,000 of our readers.

Figure 4

Now assume we set the body matter in the layout on page 21 (Figure 2) in this frequently used sans serif face, Helvetica. The chances now are that the message will be comprehended thoroughly by only 120,000 of our readers.

A sample of Helvetica, a sans serif typeface.

So we'll revert to a roman face, but this time we'll play about a little with the headline, placing it about halfway down the body matter, as in Figure 5 (next page). The number of our readers who show good comprehension of the message zooms to 320,000—but we're still only halfway back to square one.

So we'll go back to Figure 2, but this time we'll introduce a new element. We'll put the headline in a high chroma color, say hot red, or process red.

The introduction of spot color immediately boosts our potential readership to about 1.6 million. But, sadly, this use of spot color works against comprehension to such a degree that the potential army of readers who receive our message loudly and clearly is reduced to a mere corps of about 272,000. That's 400,000 less than we started with.

And that should be enough to frighten anyone!

Figure 5

The text then starts here and continues without interruption in this three-column layout. Text is fully justified. This layout is the sort called Ayer No. 1. It is much favored in advertising circles. It is also found in magazines and newspapers—although most layout artists frown on such obvious simplicity.

The text then starts here and continues without interruption in this three-column layout. Text is fully justified. This layout is the sort called Ayer No. 1. It is much favored in advertising circles. It is also found in magazines and newspapers—although most layout artists frown on such obvious simplicity.

layout is the sort called Ayer No. 1. It is much favored in advertising circles. It is also found in magazines and newspapers—although most layout artists frown on such obvious simplicity.

The text then starts here and continues without interruption in this three-column layout. Text is fully justified. This layout is the sort called Ayer No. 1. It is much favored in advertising circles. It is also found in magazines and newspapers—although most layout artists frown on such obvious simplicity.

The text then starts here and continues without interruption in this three-column layout. Text is fully justified. This

newspapers—although most layout artists frown on such obvious simplicity.

The text then starts here and continues without interruption in this three-column layout. Text is fully justified. This layout is the sort called Ayer No. 1. It is much favored in advertising circles. It is also found in magazines and newspapers—although most layout artists frown on such obvious simplicity.

The text then starts here and continues without interruption in this three-column layout. Text is fully justified. This layout is the sort called Ayer No. 1. It is much favored in advertising circles. It is also found in magazines and

The Headline Goes Here, Dividing the Text

The text then starts here and continues without interruption in this three-column layout. Text is fully justified. This layout is the sort called Ayer No. 1. It is much favored in advertising circles. It is also found in magazines and newspapers—although most layout artists frown on such obvious simplicity.

The text then starts here and continues without interruption in this three-column layout. Text is fully justified. This layout is the sort called Ayer No. 1. It is much favored in advertising circles. It is also found in magazines and newspapers—although most layout artists frown on such obvious simplicity.

The text then starts here and continues without interruption in this three-column layout. Text is fully justified. This

layout is the sort called Ayer No. 1. It is much favored in advertising circles. It is also found in magazines and newspapers—although most layout artists frown on such obvious simplicity.

The text then starts here and continues without interruption in this three-column layout. Text is fully justified. This layout is the sort called Ayer No. 1. It is much favored in advertising circles. It is also found in magazines and newspapers—although most layout artists frown on such obvious simplicity.

The text then starts here and continues without interruption in this three-column layout. Text is fully justified. This layout is the sort called Ayer No. 1. It is much favored in advertising circles. It is also found in magazines and

newspapers—although most layout artists frown on such obvious simplicity.

The text then starts here and continues without interruption in this three-column layout. Text is fully justified. This layout is the sort called Ayer No. 1. It is much favored in advertising circles. It is also found in magazines and newspapers—although most layout artists frown on such obvious simplicity.

The text then starts here and continues without interruption in this three-column layout. Text is fully justified. This layout is the sort called Ayer No. 1. It is much favored in advertising circles. It is also found in magazines and newspapers—although most layout artists frown on such obvious simplicity.

A layout that hinders the reader.

TWO

A Beautifully Painted Square Wheel

FIFTY YEARS AGO, the eminent English typographer Stanley Morison gave this definition of his craft:

> *"Typography is the efficient means to an essentially utilitarian, and only accidentally esthetic, end, for the enjoyment of patterns is rarely the reader's chief aim."*

That quotation is included in many textbooks on typography.

Usually, however, that is as far as the quotation is taken. But Morison went on to say this:

". . . *any disposition of printing material which, what-*
ever the intention, has the effect of coming between
author and reader, is wrong."

This study is dedicated to exploring Morison's second tenet.

The intention is to show that certain typographical elements not only do not encourage reading, but actually discourage the reader by throwing unnecessary distractions in his or her path, thereby interrupting reading rhythm.

The student who browses through a collection of today's magazines could be excused for thinking that typography largely has been replaced by abstract esthetics and artistic inspiration.

Morison, it appears, has become one of yesterday's men, and with him the English academic Herbert Spencer, who said: "The true economics of printing must be measured by how much is read and understood, and not by how much is produced."

In the new wave of design, publications and advertisements are conceived in the hope their content of information will fit neatly into the artistic design created for them. Some printed materials have become merely packages created on the basis of divine inspiration. This is nonsensical.

Figure 6

edited by
Kristin Spence

Free-Netting

You might not expect the electronic frontier to run through the Florida Panhandle. But as many as 3,000 Leon County residents log onto the *Tallahassee Free-Net* each day to check community calendars, peruse the proposed state budget, access the Internet, post critiques of the new downtown parking plan, and even get an update on the activities of Quilters Unlimited of Tallahassee. "The city manager just resigned today, and I'm sure it's all over the Free-Net," said Tallahassee Free-Net co-founder Hilbert Levitz. The Tallahassee Free-Net – with 19,000 registered users in a county with a population of 200,000 – is a thriving example of this fast-growing system of open-access community computing. Rather than cater to the already-wired, Free-Nets aim to reflect and inform the populations of the cities and towns in which they are based. That local focus brings in people who might never otherwise surf the Net.

"We're basically here to prepare the community for their role in the coming National Information Infrastructure, and in that sense we're an educational endeavor," Levitz says, noting that 300 people attend Free-Net beginner's workshops each month.

Free-Nets were born in 1984, when Tom Grundner, now president of the National Public Telecomputing Network but then working at Case Western Reserve University's Department of Family Medicine, used his Apple II Plus to connect several clinics around Cleveland. Non-employees soon began logging on in hopes that doctors would answer their medical questions. "What if we devised a system that would reflect the whole community, and the hospital was just one building in that community?" Grundner wondered. His question later led to the creation of the Cleveland Free-Net Community Computer System, which now handles some 12,000 logins a day.

"Here in Cleveland, middle-class, blue-collar people are not going to get online to search the catalog at the University of Paris, but they *will* go online to see what's happening with the Cleveland Browns," says Grundner. "These systems are not run like radio and television stations, where somebody else is deciding what you're going to see and hear. They're designed by the community to fit the needs of that community."

The National Public Telecomputing Network is the hub of the Free-Net system, connecting the 34 affiliated Free-Nets already online and 100 organizing committees at work in 38 states and 6 countries. But the nonprofit, grant-supported group cannot fulfill the country's Free-Net needs, Grundner said. And so the network is pushing for legislation to establish a government-funded, independently run organization similar to the Corporation for Public Broadcasting. This "corporation for community computing" would help build and support Free-Net style networks around the country, much as the Corporation for Public Broadcasting supports public TV and radio.

Established in 1989 to spread the Free-Net gospel, the National Public Telecomputing Network now offers a variety of "cybercasting" services to its affiliates and has begun a rural outreach program to overcome structural obstacles to establishing Free-Nets in smaller communities. But the focus remains on local interest and wide access.

To learn more about the National Public Telecomputing Network, establishing a Free-Net in your community, or logging onto one that already exists, send *e-mail* to *info@nptn.org* or *ftp* to *nptn.org* and log in anonymously.

To access Tallahassee Free Net, *telnet* to *freenet.fsu.edu* (144.174.128.43) or modem to +1 (904) 488 5056, parity none, character length 8, one stop bit, vt100 or vt102.

– *Joel Brown* joel711@delphi.com.

125

Was this magazine communicating with its readers
–or just making pretty shapes?

Design is not, or should not be, mere decoration and abstraction, but part of the business of communication.

The concern should not be for the beholder's—or creator's—eye for beauty. It should be for those who, it is hoped, will read a publication and gain sufficiently from it to want to buy it again, or the product it advertises, or both.

But how frequently are opinions on the invalidity of a typographic design cast aside, displaced by the view that legibility isn't important if the product looks exciting?

This is absurd. A design that looks exciting but is incomprehensible is nothing more than a beautifully painted square wheel!

Newspapers, magazines, and advertisements should be vehicles for transmitting ideas, and their design should be an integral part of that process, and forever under scrutiny.

Good design is a blend of function and form, and the greater of these is function. This is as true of typography as it is of an opera house or a space shuttle.

Typography fails if it allows the reader's interest to decline. It fails absolutely if it contributes to the destruction of the reader's interest.

It's easy to accept Morison's dictum that any design which comes between author and reader is wrong. What is not so easy is to identify those typographical elements that are flawed.

Figure 7

Term	Serif Example	Sans Serif Example
serif	This type has serifs.	
sans serif		This type doesn't.
roman	Roman type.	
normal		Normal type.
italic	*This is italic.*	
oblique		*This is oblique.*
small capitals	SMALL CAPITALS.	HERE, TOO!
capitals	TRUE CAPITALS.	TRUE CAPITALS.

Typographical terminology illustrated.

There is wider agreement now on some design factors, such as that serif body type and lower case headlines are easier to read than their opposite numbers, but this agreement is little more than lip service. The millennium, as English author and journalist Harold Evans put it, is not yet upon us.

Quantitative research has been hard to come by, and, robbed of the benefits of empiricism, we are forced to rely on what we know instinctively to be right. Regrettably, our instincts, reinforced though they may be by practical training, can lead us horribly astray.

The distinguished American typographer and teacher Edmund Arnold points out that reading as a learned skill has suffered much from the failure of the school system. Surveys, he says, have shown that the typical American high school graduate has a reading skill comparable to that expected of a sixth grade student.

With this drop in reading proficiency, Arnold says, young people have become more attuned to television, which requires neither audience participation nor an attention span.

If newspapers are to continue to prosper, they must replace their aging readers with converts from the television-dominated generation. For them, the process of reading must be as painless and physically undemanding as possible.

A would-be reader, faced with a difficult task demanding physical skill and concentration that he or she lacks, is inclined to reach for the crutch of broadcast news and ideas. And even the expert reader has a limited time each day for gathering information. Typography must ensure that none of this valuable time, plus the concomitant energy and concentration, is wasted.

Devices that lead a reader on a wild goose chase, disturb an efficient pattern, or cause the slightest measure of distress, should, Arnold says, be eliminated.

Arnold insists on design that pays tribute to the linearity of the Latin alphabet and the physiology of the act of reading.

When we're taught to read, we're told to start at the top left corner of the reading matter and work our way across and down, going from left to right and back again, until we reach the bottom right corner.

Arnold has devised what he calls the Gutenberg Diagram, illustrated in Figure 8 (next page), the principles of which, he says, all design should respect.

Arnold says the eyes fall naturally to the top left corner, which he calls the Primary Optical Area (POA). Then the eyes move across and down the page, obeying reading gravity, and returning after each left-to-right sweep to an Axis of Orientation.

Any design that forces the reader to work against reading gravity, or fails to return him or her to a logical Axis of Orientation, tends to destroy reading rhythm and should, he asserts, be outlawed.

But the question is: is Arnold right? Where is the research that quantifies his assertions? And what of all the other maxims, axioms, and unwritten laws of printing and design that are handed down from printer to apprentice, from editor to cadet, from creative or art director to advertising trainee, like tablets of stone?

Where's the research that quantifies the supposed supremacy of serif body type over sans and of lower case headlines over capitals? And are headlines in spot color really counterproductive, and to what extent?

Figure 8

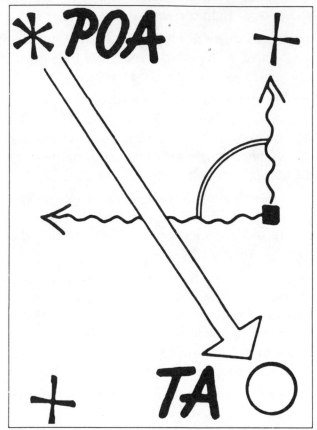

Gutenberg Diagram charts basic reading eye movement
from the Primary Optical Area (POA)
to the Terminal Anchor (TA). Crosses indicate
fallow corners and the arc of wavy lines shows
"backward" movement that the reading eye resists.

Much work has been done on research into the legibility of typefaces, particularly in the early part of this century. But very little appears to have been done outside the laboratory, and, more importantly, among those who buy and consume the printed word.

After a fruitless six-month search for detailed research material, I determined to conduct my own research program into the comprehensibility of reading matter, in an attempt to isolate and measure those type elements which, when used in apparently ill-considered ways, could deter, disenchant, or even antagonize the reader.

Before doing so, I sought the advice of research consultants and academics in the United States, Britain, and Australia, and submitted my proposed methodology, and later the results, to them for reservation, comment, or dissent. The consensus: that the study was both valid and valuable for students and practitioners of typography and graphic design. (Please see the Appendix for more information about the methodology.)

Figure 9

The Headline Goes Up Here

The text then starts here and continues without interruption in this four-column layout. Text is fully justified. This layout is much favored by readers—and much less so by magazine and newspaper editors, not to mention advertising people. Most layout artists frown on such obvious simplicity. Who's in the right?

The layout in this figure complies with Edmund Arnold's Gutenberg Diagram. In reading comprehension tests, it was contrasted with a layout, shown as Figure 10, which defies the principles Arnold has enunciated. The layout in this figure complies with Edmund Arnold's Gutenberg Diagram. In reading comprehension tests, it was contrasted with a layout, shown as Figure 10, which defies the principles Arnold has enunciated. The text then starts here and continues without interruption in this four-column layout. Text is fully justified. This layout is much favored by readers—and much less so by magazine and newspaper editors, not to mention advertising people. Most layout artists frown on such obvious simplicity. Who's in the right?

The layout in this figure complies with Edmund Arnold's Gutenberg Diagram. In reading comprehension tests, it was contrasted with a layout, shown as Figure 10, which defies the principles Arnold has enunciated. The layout in this figure complies with Edmund Arnold's Gutenberg Diagram. In reading comprehension tests, it was contrasted with a layout, shown as Figure 10, which defies the principles Arnold has enunciated. The text then starts here and continues without interruption in this four-column layout. Text is fully justified. This layout is much favored by readers—and much less so by magazine and newspaper editors, not to mention adver-

tising people. Most layout artists frown on such obvious simplicity. Who's in the right?

The layout in this figure complies with Edmund Arnold's Gutenberg Diagram. In reading comprehension tests, it was contrasted with a layout, shown as Figure 10, which defies the principles Arnold has enunciated. The layout in this figure complies with Edmund Arnold's Gutenberg Diagram. In reading comprehension tests, it was contrasted with a layout, shown as Figure 10, which defies the principles Arnold has enunciated. The text then starts here and continues without interruption in this four-column layout. Text is fully justified. This layout is much favored by readers—and much less so by magazine and newspaper editors, not to mention advertising people. Most layout artists frown on such obvious simplicity. Who's in the right?

The layout in this figure complies with Edmund Arnold's Gutenberg Diagram. In

reading comprehension tests, it was contrasted with a layout, shown as Figure 10, which defies the principles Arnold has enunciated. The layout in this figure complies with Edmund Arnold's Gutenberg Diagram. In reading comprehension tests, it was contrasted with a layout, shown as Figure 10, which defies the principles Arnold has enunciated. The layout in this figure complies with Edmund Arnold's Gutenberg Diagram. In reading comprehension tests, it was contrasted with a layout, shown as Figure 10, which defies the principles Arnold has enunciated. The text then starts here and continues without interruption in this four-column layout. Text is fully justified. This layout is much favored by readers—and much less so by magazine and newspaper editors, not to mention advertising people. Most layout artists frown on such obvious simplicity. Who's in the right?

The layout in this figure complies with Edmund Arnold's Gutenberg Diagram. In reading comprehension tests, it was contrasted with a layout, shown as Figure 10, which defies the principles Arnold has enunciated. The layout in this figure complies with Edmund Arnold's Gutenberg Diagram. In reading comprehension tests, it was contrasted with a layout, shown as Figure 10, which defies the principles Arnold has enunciated. The text then starts here and continues without interruption in this four-column layout. Text is fully justified. This layout is much favored by readers—and much less so by magazine and newspaper editors, not to mention advertising people. Most layout artists frown on such obvious simplicity. Who's in the right?

The layout in this figure complies with Edmund Arnold's Gutenberg Diagram. In reading comprehension tests, it was contrasted with a layout, shown as Figure 10, which defies the principles Arnold has enunciated. The layout in this figure complies with Edmund Arnold's Gutenberg Diagram. In reading comprehension tests, it was contrasted with a layout, shown as Figure 10, which defies the principles Arnold has enunciated. The text then starts here and continues without interruption in this four-column layout. Text is fully justified. This layout is much favored by readers—and much less so by magazine and newspaper editors, not to mention advertising people. Most layout artists frown on such obvious simplicity. Who's in the right?

tising people. Most layout artists frown on such obvious simplicity. Who's in the right?

The layout in this figure complies with Edmund Arnold's Gutenberg Diagram. In reading comprehension tests, it was contrasted with a layout, shown as Figure 10, which defies the principles Arnold has enunciated. The layout in this figure complies with Edmund Arnold's Gutenberg Diagram. In reading comprehension tests, it was contrasted with a layout, shown as Figure 10, which defies the principles Arnold has enunciated. The text then starts here and continues without interruption in this four-column layout. Text is fully justified. This layout is much favored by readers—and much less so by magazine and newspaper editors, not to mention advertising people. Most layout artists frown on such obvious simplicity. Who's in the right?

The layout in this figure complies with Edmund Arnold's Gutenberg Diagram. In reading comprehension tests, it was contrasted with a layout, shown as Figure 10, which defies the principles Arnold has enunciated. The layout in this figure complies with Edmund Arnold's Gutenberg Diagram. In reading comprehension tests, it was contrasted with a layout, shown as Figure 10, which defies the principles Arnold has enunciated. The text then starts here and continues without interruption in this four-column layout. Text is fully justified. This layout is much favored by readers—and much less so by magazine and newspaper editors, not to mention advertising people. Most layout artists frown on such obvious simplicity. Who's in the right? The layout in this figure complies with Edmund Arnold's Gutenberg Diagram. In reading comprehension tests, it was contrasted with the layout in Figure 10, which defies Arnold. As Figure 10 the principles Arnold has enunciated. Most layout artists frown on such obvious simplicity. Who's in the right? The layout in this figure complies with Edmund Arnold's Gutenberg Diaddafewxxxagram. In replies Arnold has enunciated. ■

A layout that acknowledges reading gravity.

§ *THREE*

The Perils of Ignoring Gravity

THE FIRST PRECEPT examined was the positional relationship of headlines to body matter: whether the irregular
placement of headlines could cause a break in reading rhythm
strong enough to affect the reader's concentration.

The layout in Figure 9 (opposite page) complies with
Arnold's Gutenberg Diagram. It was contrasted with the
layout shown as Figure 10 (on page 39), which defies the
principles he has enunciated.

On any page where there is writing or printing, the
starting point is the upper left corner. Here the eye, trained

from babyhood, enters a page, and here it must be caught by an attention-compeller. When the eye reaches the lower right corner, after scanning across and down progressively, the reading task is finished. Reading gravity doesn't follow a straight line. It moves to right and left, and has to be lured to what are called the fallow corners by optical magnets, usually illustrations.

The eye does not willingly go against reading gravity, with the obvious exception that, having read a line of type or writing, it returns to the beginning of that line to begin the succeeding line.

The point to which the eye returns, automatically, is the point at which the line began. Any variation from this causes an interruption to reading rhythm. Arnold calls the point to which the eye returns the Axis of Orientation. He maintains that if this axis is altered by typographical means, the eye is likely to rebel, and a reader may become an ex-reader.

Figure 10

The layout in this figure defies Edmund Arnold's Gutenberg Diagram. In reading comprehension tests, it was contrasted with a layout, shown as Figure 9, which complies the principles Arnold has enunciated. The layout in this figure defies Edmund Arnold's Gutenberg Diagram. In reading comprehension tests, it was contrasted with a layout, shown as Figure 9, which complies with the principles Arnold has enunciated.

The layout in this figure defies Edmund Arnold's Gutenberg Diagram. In reading comprehension tests, it was contrasted with a layout, shown as Figure 9, which complies with the principles Arnold has enunciated.he layout in this figure The layout in this figure complies with Edmund Arnold's Gutenberg Diagram. In reading comprehension tests, it was contrasted with a layout, shown as Figure 10, which defies the principles Arnold has enunciated.

The layout in this figure complies with Edmund Arnold's Gutenberg Diagram. In reading comprehension tests, it was contrasted with a layout, shown as Figure 10, which defies the principles Arnold has enunciated.

The layout in this figure complies with Edmund Arnold's Gutenberg Diagram. In reading comprehension tests, it was contrasted with a layout, shown as Figure 10, which defies the principles Arnold has enunciated.The layout in this figure defies Edmund Arnold's Gutenberg Diagram. In reading comprehension tests, it was contrasted with a layout, shown as Figure 9, which complies with the principles Arnold has enunciated.he layout in this figure The layout in this figure complies with Edmund Arnold's Gutenberg Diagram. In reading comprehension tests, it was contrasted with a layout, shown as Figure 10, which defies the principles Arnold has enunciated.

The layout in this figure complies with Edmund Arnold's Gutenberg Diagram. In reading comprehension tests, it was contrasted with a layout, shown as Figure 10, which defies the principles Arnold has enunciated.

The layout in this figure complies with

The Headline Goes Here, in the Center

Edmund Arnold's Gutenberg Diagram. In reading comprehension tests, it was contrasted with a layout, shown as Figure 10, which defies the principles Arnold has enunciated.The layout in this figure defies Edmund Arnold's Gutenberg Diagram. In reading comprehension tests, it was contrasted with a layout, shown as Figure 9, which complies with the principles Arnold has enunciated.he layout in this figure The layout in this figure complies with Edmund Arnold's Gutenberg Diagram. In reading comprehension tests, it was contrasted with a layout, shown as Figure 10, which defies the principles Arnold has enunciated.

The layout in this figure complies with Edmund Arnold's Gutenberg Diagram. In reading comprehension tests, it was contrasted with a layout, shown as Figure 10, which defies the principles Arnold has enunciated.

The layout in this figure complies with

Edmund Arnold's Gutenberg Diagram. In reading comprehension tests, it was contrasted with a layout, shown as Figure 10, which defies the principles Arnold has enunciated.The layout in this figure defies Edmund Arnold's Gutenberg Diagram. In reading comprehension tests, it was contrasted with a layout, shown as Figure 9, which complies with the principles Arnold has enunciated.he layout in this figure The layout in this figure complies with Edmund Arnold's Gutenberg Diagram. In reading comprehension tests, it was contrasted with a layout, shown as Figure 10, which defies the principles Arnold has enunciated.

The layout in this figure complies with Edmund Arnold's Gutenberg Diagram. In reading comprehension tests, it was contrasted with a layout, shown as Figure 10, which defies the principles Arnold has enunciated.The layout in this figure complies with Edmund Arnold's Gutenberg Diagram. In reading comprehension tests, it was contrasted with a layout, shown as Figure 10, which defies the principles Arnold has enunciated.The layout in this figure complies with Edmund Arnold's Gutenberg Diagram. In reading comprehension tests, it was contrasted with a layout, shown as Figure 10, which defies the principles Arnold has enunciated.he layout in this figure The layout in this figure complies with Edmund Arnold's Gutenberg Diagram. In reading comprehension tests, it was contrasted with a layout, shown as Figure 10, which defies the principles Arnold has enunciated.The layout in this figure complies with Edmund Arnold's Gutenberg Diagram. In reading comprehension tests, it was contrasted with a layout, shown as Figure 10, which defies the principles Arnold has enunciated.

The layout in this figure complies with Edmund Arnold's Gutenberg Diagram, rasted with a layout, shown as Figure 10, which defies the principles Arnold has enunciated.The layout in this figure complies with Edmund Arnold's Gutenberg Diagram. rasted with a layout, shown as Figure 10, which defies the principles Arnold has enunciated. trasted with a layout, shown as Figure 10, which defies the principles Arnold has enunciated.

The layout in this figure complies with Edmund Arnold's Gutenberg Diagram. In reading comprehension tests, it was contrasted with a layout, shown as Figure 10, which defies the principles Arnold has enunciated.The layout in this figure defies Edmund Arnold's Gutenberg Diagram. In reading comprehension tests, it was contrasted with a layout, shown as Figure 9, which complies with the principles Arnold has enunciated.he layout in this figure The layout in this figure complies with Edmund Arnold's Gutenberg Diagram. In reading comprehension tests, it was contrasted with a layout, shown as Figure 9, which complies with the principles Arnold has enunciated.

The layout in this figure complies with Edmund Arnold's Gutenberg Diagram. In reading comprehension tests, it was contrasted with a layout, shown as Figure 10, which defies the principles Arnold has enunciated.The layout in this figure complies with Edmund Arnold's Gutenberg Diagram. In reading comprehension tests, it was contrasted with a layout, shown as Figure 10, which defies the principles Arnold has enunciated.The layout in this figure complies with Edmund Arnold's Gutenberg Diagram. In reading comprehension tests, it was contrasted with a layout, shown as Figure 10, which defies the principles Arnold has enunciated.he layout in this figure The layout in this figure complies with Edmund Arnold's Gutenberg Diagram. In reading comprehension tests, it was contrasted with a layout, shown as Figure 9, which complies with the principles Arnold has enunciated.he layout in this figure The layout in this figure complies with Edmund Arnold's Gutenberg Diagram. In reading comprehension tests, it was contrasted with a layout, shown as Figure 10, which defies the principles Arnold has enunciated.

The layout in this figure complies with Edmund Arnold's Gutenberg Diagram, rasted with a layout, shown as Figure 10, which defies the principles Arnold has enunciated.The layout in this figure complies with Edmund Arnold's Gutenberg Diagram. rasted with a layout, shown as Figure 10, which defies the principles Arnold has enunciated. trasted with a layout, shown as Figure 10, which defies the principles Arnold has enunciated.

A layout that ignores reading gravity.

In Figure 9, it will be seen that the eye falls naturally to the headline, and, the principle of the Axis of Orientation being obeyed, would fall to the introduction, then follow naturally the flow of the body type. The two pieces of half-tone illustration act as magnets to the fallow corners, and the sign-off logotype acts as the Terminal Anchor.

In Figure 10, instead of being attracted by the headline to the top left corner, the eyes are attracted by the headline to a point below the upper illustration. Having read the headline, the eyes want to observe the principles of reading gravity and the Axis of Orientation, and fall to the small leg of type in the second column. This obviously will make little or no sense.

The eye then is forced to make the journey against reading gravity to the Primary Optical Area to begin the article. The reading rhythm has been destroyed, and, as the research program shows, considerable damage may have been done to the reader's comprehension of the article.

In the research program, the readers were subjected to an equal mix of both types of layout. Headlines in each instance were 42 point Helvetica bold lower case, two decks, set over 27 picas. (See Figure 11 on the opposite page.) Body type was eight on nine point Corona lower case over 12.5 picas. Illustrations and captions were of identical size on each layout. Layouts were four columns, 12.5 picas wide and 30 centimeters deep—a total body type area, pictures excluded, of about 65 centimeters.

Figure 11

Headlines Like This

Body copy in articles used in the research looked a lot like this. Corona is similar to this typeface (Century Old style). And this text is set eight on nine point over 12.5 picas, as was the text in the research. Body copy in articles used in the research looked a lot like this. Corona is similar to this typeface (Century Oldstyle). And this text is set eight on nine point over 12.5 picas, as was the text in the research.

The types chosen were selected because of their potentially high legibility. The criteria for this were optical rather than geometric design; easily discernible differences between letters; and greater x-heights than available alternatives.

The layout in Figure 10 contained one design element not used in Figure 9. In an attempt to induce readers to make the jump against reading gravity from the second deck of the headline to the introductory paragraph, a drop cap was used. In Figure 9, an initial drop cap was not used because of the likelihood that it would clash with the headline.

The figures presented in Table 1 are expressed as percentages of readers achieving the comprehension levels shown, as an average of all tests.

Table 1

	Comprehension Level		
	Good	Fair	Poor
Layout complying with principles of reading gravity	67	19	14
Layout disregarding reading gravity	32	30	38

The levels of comprehension of articles of direct interest were within five percentage points above the average, and those of specific or limited interest, within five percentage points below the average. This, with one statistically insignificant variation, was the norm for all tests in the entire program.

Following the formal questions, readers were invited to comment on what they had read, and on the way it was presented. None of those who registered high comprehension commented on the design. However, many who scored poorly with Figure 10 layouts said they found they were conscious of having to find their way to the beginning of the story—the eyes fell naturally to the leg of type in column two, instead of making the journey back to the top of column one. Yet those same people scored well in comprehension when reading similar articles in the Figure 9 layouts.

Of those who scored "poor," a high proportion answered correctly the questions linked to the early part of the articles, then failed to score correctly again. Similarly, those who scored "fair" generally achieved their correct answers among the four to six questions relating to the early part of articles, then apparently failed to read on, or did so in a cursory manner.

This supports the contention that readers who are faced with a journey against reading gravity unconsciously find the effort demanding, and do not read an article with the same easy concentration as do those whose reading rhythm has not been disturbed.

At the conclusion of these tests using formal layouts such as might be used in newspapers, a supplementary test was made using free layouts, as might be used in magazines.

The body matter was set in nine on 10 Corona roman over 15 picas, and a more leisurely headline type, 72 point Bauhaus Bold lower case with a kicker line of 24 point Bauhaus Medium lower case, was used. (See Figure 12, next page.)

Figure 12

kicker

Head

Body matter in magazine articles used in the
research looked a lot like this. It was set in nine
on 10 point Corona roman, much like this Century
Oldstyle. Body matter in magazine articles used
in the research looked a lot like this. It was set in
nine on 10 point Corona roman, much like this
Century Oldstyle. Body matter in magazine
articles used in the research looked a lot like this.
It was set in nine on 10 point Corona roman, much
like this Century Oldstyle.

The layouts are shown as Figure 13 (opposite page), a
design complying with the principles of reading gravity, and
Figure 14 (following page), a design ignoring those principles.
In Figure 14, an initial drop cap was again used in an attempt
to draw the reader's attention from the headline to the introductory paragraph.

Only one type of article was used in this test, as opposed
to the two in the major test. The articles were similar in
content, and had the common theme of domestic tourism,

Figure 13

Kicker Up
Here

Two-Deck
Headline

The layout in this figure complies with Edmund Arnold's Gutenberg Diagram. In reading comprehension tests, it was contrasted with a layout, shown as Figure 10, which defies the principles Arnold has enunciated. The layout in this figure complies with Edmund Arnold's Gutenberg Diagram. In reading comprehension tests, it was contrasted with a layout, shown as Figure 10, which defies the principles Arnold has enunciated.

The layout in this figure complies with Edmund Arnold's Gutenberg Diagram. In reading comprehension tests, it was contrasted with a layout, shown as Figure 10, which defies the principles Arnold has enunciated.

The layout in this figure complies with Edmund Arnold's Gutenberg Diagram. In reading comprehension tests, it was contrasted with a layout, shown as Figure 10, which defies the principles Arnold has enunciated.

The layout in this figure complies with Edmund Arnold's Gutenberg Diagram. The layout in this figure complies with Edmund Arnold's Gutenberg Diagram. The layout in this figure defes Edmund Arnold's Gutenberg Diagram. In reading comprehension tests, it was contrasted with a layout, shown as Figure 9, which complies with the principles Arnold has

enunciated.he layout in this figure The layout in this figure defes Edmund Arnold's Gutenberg Diagram. rasted with a layout, shown as Figure 9, which complies with the principles Arnold has enunciated.he layout in this figure he layout in this figure defes Edmund Arnold's Gutenberg Diagram. ntrasted with a layout, shown as Figure 9, which complies with the principles Arnoldas this ends with a TA. articles used in the research began in the second column and continued into the third, where it concluded with a logotype that served as a terminal anchor. The layout in this figure complies with Edmund gram. In reading comprehension tests, it was contrasted with a layout, shown eples Arnold has enunciated. Tagram. In reading comprehension tests, it was contrasted with a layout, shown as Figure 10, which defies the principles Arnold has enunciated. in this figure complies with Edmund Arnold's Gutenberg Diagram. In reading comprehension tests, it was contrasted with a layout, shown as Figure 10, which defies the principles Arnold has served as a terminal anchor. The layout in this figure complies with Edmund gram. In reading comprehension tests, it was contrasted

A magazine layout that
acknowledges reading gravity.

a topic shown in magazine reader attitude surveys to have wide appeal. The results showed a marked similarity to the results achieved in that part of the major test employing articles of direct interest.

Figure 14

Text in magazine articles used in the research began in the second column and continued into the third, where it concluded with a logotype that served as a terminal anchor. Text in magazine articles used in the research began in the second column and continued into the third, where it concluded with a logotype that served as a terminal anchor. Text in magazine articles used in the research began in the second column and continued into the third, where it concluded with a logotype that served as a terminal anchor. Text in magazine articles used in the research began in the second column and continued into the third, where it concluded with a logotype that served as a terminal anchor. Text in magazine articles used in the research began in the second column and continued into the third, where it concluded with a logotype that served as a terminal anchor. Text in magazine articles used in the research began in the second column and continued into the

third, where it concluded with a logotype that served as a terminal anchor. Text in magazine articles used in the research began in the second column and continued into the third, where it concluded with a logotype that served as a terminal anchor. Text in magazine articles used in the research began in the second column and continued into the third, where it concluded with a logotype that served as a terminal anchor. Text in magazine articles used in the research began in the second column and continued into the third, where it concluded with a logotype that served as a terminal anchor. Text in magazine articles used in the research began in the second column and continued into the third, where it concluded with a logotype that served as a terminal anchor. Text in magazine articles used in the research began in the second column and continued into the third, where it concluded mrinal anchor. Text in magazine articles used in the research began in the second column and

continued into the third, where it concluded with a logotype that served as a terminal anchor. Text in magazine articles used in the research began in the second column and continued into the third, where it concluded mrinal anchor. Text in magazine articles used in the second column and continued into the third, where it concluded with a logotype that served as a terminal anchor. Text in magazine articles used in the research began in the second.

Headline Down Here   Kicker Here

A magazine layout that ignores reading gravity.

In the test using Figure 13, 73 per cent of readers showed good comprehension, 21 per cent showed fair comprehension, and 6 per cent poor comprehension.

In the test using Figure 14, 37 per cent showed good comprehension, 31 per cent showed fair comprehension, and 32 per cent poor comprehension.

The comparison between these results and the results of the formal layout relating to articles of direct interest is shown below in Table 2.

Table 2

	Comprehension Level		
	Good	Fair	Poor
Layout complying with principles of reading gravity			
Formal layout	72	20	8
Free layout	73	21	6
Layout disregarding reading gravity			
Formal layout	34	31	35
Free layout	37	31	32

Remember that the layouts used in Figures 10 and 14—those that disregarded reading gravity—were given a typographical crutch in the shape of an initial drop cap on the introductory paragraph. Even with a crutch these layouts failed in their objective, so it was not considered necessary to calculate how much further they might have failed had this crutch been removed.

The conclusion to be drawn must be that designs that conform to natural reading physiology are largely acceptable to readers. Those that don't conform run the risk of going largely unread.

The advertisement shown in Figure 15 (opposite page) was published in a technical trade magazine.

The danger created in its design is that the reader's eyes will be drawn to the headline, a false Primary Optical Area, then will fall naturally to the copy beneath. This will be confusing. The risk is that the reader will, at best, work against reading gravity to find the beginning of the copy, or at worst, give up and turn the page.

But here's a potential disaster area. In the research program, many of the readers who made the journey against reading gravity found the task exhausting in some way, and some read only two or three paragraphs before losing interest.

And if the offer being promoted is in the fifth of six paragraphs, as with Figure 15, that's tough luck.

Figure 15

*The position of this headline
could confuse the reader.*

Figure 16 (opposite page) is another example of ill-considered design. The headline attracts the eye, which then falls to the text immediately below the headline in the third column. This makes no sense.

This ad, which appeared in a widely read business magazine, sports a clever, four-color illustration. It's well-written. And I can't quarrel with the choice of typefaces.

But whether this advertisement succeeded in communicating its message is, I submit, highly questionable.

So having determined that the simple design style, shown in Figure 9, was acceptable to most readers, I retained it for the remainder of the program, and discarded Figure 10.

Conclusion

¶   *The influence of reading gravity is substantial. More than twice as many readers will readily understand text presented in a layout complying with the principles of reading gravity than one defying reading gravity.*

Figure 16

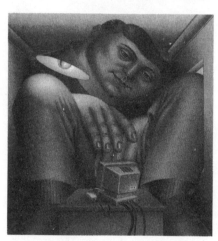

Here, the reader is faced with too many decisions.

FOUR

Serif versus Sans Serif Body Type

WHICH IS EASIER TO READ: serif or sans serif body type? On this question there appears to be complete polarization.

There are few major newspapers today that use sans serif type for the body text. Conversely, many major magazines choose sans serif.

Serif faces have long been regarded as highly readable. One theory was that the serifs acted as tramlines, keeping the eyes on target. Another was that the modulated thick and thin strokes of serif types provided greater opportunity for

individual letters, and hence words, to be distinguished and
read.

Figure 17

abcdefghijklmnopqrstuvwxyz
ABCDEFGHIJKLMNOPQRST
UVWXYZ1234567890!@#$%^
&*()_+|-=\<>?,./

A serif typeface (ITC New Baskerville),
with thick and thin strokes.

Above, Figure 17 shows a serif type, with its thick and
thin strokes and terminal serifs. Figure 18 on the next page
shows a sans serif face with its almost uniform strokes and
absence of serifs.

Figure 18

abcdefghijklmnopqrstuvw
xyzABCDEFGHIJKLMNOP
QRSTUVWXYZ123456789
0!@#$%^&*()_+|

A sans serif typeface (Futura Extra Black),
with monotonal strokes and no serifs.

Not all serif faces, nor all sans serif faces, share similar characteristics, as you can see in Figure 19 (next page). Caslon Openface, for example, is vastly different from Times New Roman. Optima, an optically-designed face, with considerable variation in the stroke thickness of individual letters, is vastly different from the geometric, theoretical Futura, with its identical strokes and bowls. But Caslon Openface and Futura are unlikely—one hopes—to be chosen as body types, and so the terms serif and sans serif are taken to refer to those types generally used in text by newspapers, magazines, and advertising agencies.

Figure 19

This sentence is set in Caslon Openface.

This sentence is set in Times Roman.

This sentence is set in Optima.

This sentence is set in Futura.

*Four representative typefaces,
two serif and two sans serif.*

In research collated by the British Medical Council in 1926, it was asserted that the absence of serifs in sans serif body type permitted what the council referred to as irradiation, an optical effect in which space between lines of type intruded into the letters, setting up a form of light vibration, which militated against comfortable reading. Serifs, the research said, prevented this irradiation. Thus serif types were easier to read.

Magazine editors and art directors argue that sans serif body type is clean, uncluttered, and attractive.

And so it is.

But they also argue that any difficulties with comprehensibility—should they exist—will pass, as people become more and more used to seeing and reading sans serif.

People will grow to live with it, and it will soon become comprehensible to all, and all will eventually love it, they say.

This is nonsense. It's analogous to saying that instead of feeding your children wheatie pops, you should feed them wood shavings. They'll get used to them and in time will learn to love them.

Judge for yourself. Take a look at Figure 20, which appears on the next page.

In the tests on the comprehensibility of serif body matter versus sans serif, the same procedure was used as for the previous series of tests. Body type was eight point Corona on a nine point body for the serif layouts, and eight point Helvetica on a nine point body for the sans serif layouts.

Comments made by readers who showed poor comprehension of articles set in sans serif had a common theme: the difficulty in holding concentration.

Of the 112 readers who read an article of direct interest, 67 showed poor comprehension, and of these:

» 53 complained strongly about the difficulty of reading the type.

» 11 said the task caused them physical discomfort (eye tiredness).

» 32 said the type was merely hard to read.

Figure 20

Will the message in this
magazine ad come through?

» 10 said they found they had to backtrack continually to try to maintain concentration.

» 5 said when they had to backtrack to recall points made in the article they gave up trying to concentrate.

» 22 said they had difficulty focusing on the type after having read a dozen or so lines.

Some readers made two or more of the above comments.

Yet when this same group was asked immediately afterwards to read another article with a domestic theme, but set in Corona, they reported no physical difficulties, and no necessity to recapitulate to maintain concentration.

Table 3

	Comprehension Level		
	Good	Fair	Poor
Layout with serif body type	67	19	14
Layout with sans serif body type	12	23	65

Figure 21

8 POINT
ABCDEFGHIJKLMNOPQRSTUVWXYZ
abcdefghijklmnopqrstuvwxyz
9 POINT
ABCDEFGHIJKLMNOPQRSTUVWXYZ
abcdefghijklmnopqrstuvwxyz
10 POINT
ABCDEFGHIJKLMNOPQRSTUVWXYZ
abcdefghijklmnopqrstuvwxyz
12 POINT
ABCDEFGHIJKLMNOPQRSTUVWXYZ
abcdefghijklmnopqrstuvwxyz
14 POINT
ABCDEFGHIJKLMNOPQRSTUVWXYZ
abcdefghijklmnopqrstuvwxyz

Corona, a widely used newspaper typeface.

Conclusion

¶ *Body type must be set in serif type if the designer intends it to be read and understood. More than five times as many readers are likely to show good comprehension when a serif body type is used instead of a sans serif body type.*

FIVE

Headline Type

DAVID OGILVY ASSERTS that headlines are the most important part of an advertisement, because the headline can tell the reader whether he or she is a "prospect" for the topic. The same could be said with equal validity about editorial matter.

Therefore, putting the right headline on an advertisement or article in the right words, the right shape, the right style, and in the right type, demands consideration.

The right words are, patently, dependent on the context. The right style and shape are, to a degree, dependent on the agency's, newspaper's, or magazine's style, or on design considerations. The right type, whether it be sans serif or serif, roman or italic, old face or modern, capitals or lower case, set natural or kerned, should be the choice of the designer.

There seems little to debate about the relative value of sans serif and serif type in headlines.

In U.S. research cited by Arnold, sans serif has been claimed as marginally more legible than serif, but the difference was too small to be considered statistically significant.

The choice generally lies with whichever style best suits the publication or the tenor of the advertisement or article.

There is, however, much to debate about the relative value of capitals and lower case in headlines.

From the early days of newspapers until the 1950s, capital letter headlines were almost an institution. Now, 40 years later, more than 75 per cent of newspapers in the western world use lower case headlines.

Editors who favor capitals claim they give greater emphasis. Those who prefer lower case claim their preference gives greater legibility.

The latter argument is easy to accept, as the facility with which this paragraph can be read should testify.

HOWEVER, READING THIS PARAGRAPH IS A MUCH HARDER TASK. THE EYES HAVE TO GROPE FOR THE IDENTITY OF LETTERS, THENCE WORDS, TO COMPREHEND THE SENSE.

Yet, despite an apparent consensus, the practice is far from general, as a browse through almost any publication will quickly show.

Figure 22

WITH ACXIOM, YOUR CUSTOMERS ARE A PRETTY EASY READ.

You can learn more about your customers and service them better with Acxiom's on-line, integrated product, book and subscription fulfillment system, GS/2000®. It integrates critical customer information across all product lines to tell you more about your customers, letting you better meet their needs.

GS/2000® can increase your revenues by allowing you to boost renewal rates, upsell more effectively and increase response to your promotions and marketing programs.

It will also provide valuable information to your customer service area, which will improve communications with the customer – helping you build long-term and profitable relationships.

Let Acxiom help you get the most out of the information you have.

ACXIOM

301 Industrial Boulevard / Conway, Arkansas 72032 / 1-800-9ACXIOM
Fulfillment Services (Magazine Subscription, One-Shots, Continuity, Book Club and Membership) • Marketing Database • List Rental Processing •
Merge/Purge • List Cleaning • List Enhancement • Mailing Services

Headlines in capitals are all too common in magazines–and in advertisements everywhere.

Those who argue for lower case because of its apparently greater legibility have the physiology of reading on their side. When a person reads a line of type, the eye recognizes letters by the shapes of their upper halves. With lower case this is simple,

Figure 23

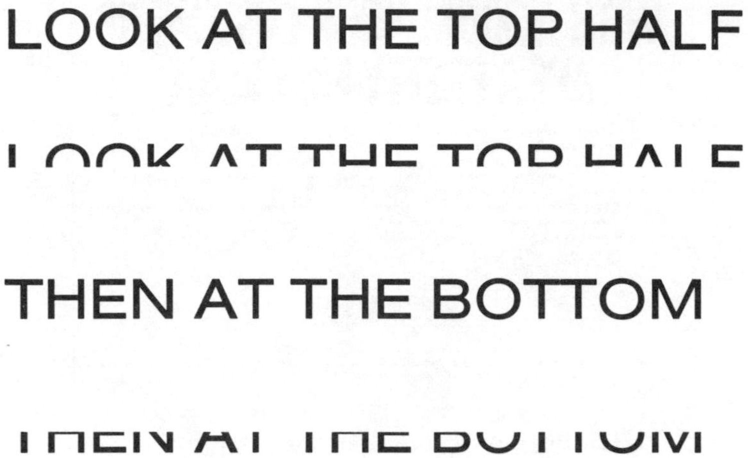

LOOK AT THE TOP HALF

LOOK AT THE TOP HALF

THEN AT THE BOTTOM

THEN AT THE BOTTOM

*The top half of letters is more recognizable
than the bottom half.*

because the top halves of lower case letters are generally distinctive, and, importantly, framed by the white space that surrounds them, permitting easy recognition.

Put the headline in capitals, and the eye is presented with a solid rectangle, and recognizing the words becomes a task instead of a natural process.

There are two factors to be considered:

» Which headline faces and styles have greater legibility?

» Do capital letter headlines have greater impact than lower case headlines, and if so, is this sufficient to counterbalance any supposed loss of legibility?

The methods used in previous tests did not lend themselves to testing the legibility of headlines, and a different method was used.

The program's 224 readers were asked during the course of the study to look at a collection of headlines, set in a variety of type styles, and were asked: "Do you find this easy to read—yes or no?"

Care was taken that surrounding type elements did not distract from the headlines. In most instances, rectangles of stick-on screen, representing illustrations, and "greek" stick-on body type were used to support the headline.

The analysis, which follows as Table 4, is expressed as percentages of the 224 readers who found the nominated headline type easy to read. Each reader was asked to pass judgment on several samples of each style. It is significant that each reader, having once declared a type easy or not easy to read, repeated that view when the same type, in a different context, was shown later in the program. Equal numbers of each style of heading were shown to the readers.

Headlines were all set 27 picas wide, in 36 point, over two decks, and in medium or bold face, depending on availability.

Table 4

Legibility of Headline Styles

1	Roman old style lower case	92%
2	Sans serif lower case	90%
3	Roman modern lower case	89%
4	Roman old style italic lower case	86%
5	Roman modern italic lower case	86%
6	Sans serif italic lower case	85%
7	Optima lower case	85%
8	Optima italic lower case	80%
9	Roman modern capitals	71%
10	Roman old style capitals	69%
11	Square serif lower case	64%
12	Roman modern italic capitals	63%
13	Roman old style italic capitals	62%
14	Sans serif italic capitals	59%
15	Optima italic capitals	57%
16	Sans serif capitals	57%
17	Optima capitals	56%
18	Square serif capitals	44%
19	Cursive or script lower case	37%
20	Ornamented lower case*	24-32%
21	Cursive or script capitals	26%
22	Ornamented capitals*	11-19%
23	Black letter lower case	10%
24	Black letter capitals	3%

*The ornamented faces came in various forms, and a range of responses is given.

Table 5

	Lower case	Capitals
Roman old style	92%	69%
Roman modern	89%	71%
Sans serif	90%	57%
Optima	85%	56%
Square serif	64%	44%

The difference in perceived legibility between capitals and lower case of the same type family is significant, as you can see from the examples shown in Table 5 above.

Optima, a humanist face designed in 1958, was included as a style in its own right out of curiosity. (Arnold cites research which claims Optima has high legibility.) It's a hybrid, having the thick and thin strokes of a serif face, yet is a sans. Essentially it's a serif face with terminals lopped off, as will be seen in Figure 24 (next page): a serif face simplified.

Figure 24

Optima is a humanist face: no serifs, but with thick and thin strokes.

Sample of Optima.

It's questionable whether a designer can simplify a serif typeface by cutting off its serifs. If one can simplify a man by cutting off his hands and feet, then so be it. Perhaps Optima's position in Table 4 answers the question.

There remains now the question of impact: whether capitals have a perceived impact great enough to counter the apparent loss in legibility.

I asked the readers to offer opinions on the perceived difference of impact. Sixteen per cent said capitals had greater impact. Fifteen per cent said lower case had greater impact. The remaining 69 per cent could see no difference in impact.

Table 4 refers to type set natural, or spaced as it comes. The effect of kerning, or minus spacing, was also considered.

The proliferation of photo-composition, aided by computers, enables modern day typesetters to do things with type that neither their predecessors, the hand and machine compositors, nor the typographers who designed the type, could have imagined.

Type can be bent around corners or in circles for display advertising purposes. It can be squeezed or stretched horizontally or vertically. The possibilities are vast. But, regrettably, this typographical horn of plenty contains some questionable fruit, as you can see in Figure 25 (next page).

Kerning is one of these.

A kern in the days of hot metal or hand-set type was that part of a type letter which protruded above, below, or to the side of the type body, e.g., the curved finial of the letter f. Now it's a photo-composition process, which gives the operator the ability to control precisely inter-letter spacing less than that of natural setting.

With kerning, individual letters such as A and W can be closed up to the adjoining letter to obtain optically even letter spacing.

Kerning is done in units, from one to three, or in extreme circumstances, four.

It's difficult to discern whether kerning is used for esthetic reasons, or because the headline writer wants another letter space or so to enable him to put his message across without having to use a condensed face or a smaller font. In most instances it appears to be purely for effect.

Figure 25

In
research
centers
around the
world, small is big.
In search of
knowledge, scientists
have discovered the
fascination of focusing on
incredibly small units. Results
often point the way to progress in
medicine, technology and other fields. ❦
At the Weizmann Institute of Science in
Rehovot, Israel, appreciation of the small is
dramatically evident in studies ranging from
elementary particles to neurotransmitters. ❦ For
example, in basic medical research Weizmann
cancer scientists participate in the front ranks
of the international search for tumor suppressor
genes to neutralize cancer-inducing oncogenes.
Elsewhere, Weizmann researchers developing
vaccinations for autoimmune diseases
(multiple sclerosis, lupus, rheumatoid
arthritis, juvenile diabetes) are carrying their

SMALL IS   studies from the cell level to the molecular
level. At the same time, scientists in the new   **BIG**
Submicron Research Center of the Institute
are handling crystal growths of layers no more
than a few atoms thick. In addition to breaking
ground in quantum physics, they expect to
develop revolutionary tools for the next
industrial age . . . such as stunningly smaller and
faster computer chips. ❦ Inevitably, at all
institutions, researchers committed to "small"
studies require major facilities. Supporting them
will open new doors to health and prosperity.

The Weizmann Institute, founded in 1934, is a
community of 2,300 scientists, engineers
and scientists-in-training engaged in a
full agenda of 800 research projects
ranging from basic medical
research in cancer, AIDS,
neurosciences and
children's diseases to
chemistry, physics,
agriculture,
mathematics
and the
environ-
ment.

AMERICAN COMMITTEE FOR THE WEIZMANN INSTITUTE OF SCIENCE
51 Madison Avenue, New York, NY 10010   212/779-2500

This ad undoubtedly attracted attention.
But how many readers tackled the text?

As more kerning units are employed, the danger increases that letters become welded together.

It must be asked whether kerning has an effect on type comprehensibility, and at what stage does the effect begin.

To test this, two types were chosen from those families which registered highest in the headline legibility test. The types, Times Roman and Helvetica, were set in 36 point capitals and lower case, bold, set naturally, and kerned one, two, three and four units, as in Figure 26 (next page).

The procedure was identical to the previous headline legibility test.

The test showed that one unit kerning had little effect on legibility. It decreased legibility in serif type, and increased it in sans serif, but minimally in each case.

Kerning two and three units had a much more pronounced effect, particularly on the legibility of serif type.

But kern four units, or to the stage where letters merge, and the reader is in dire trouble.

Compounding the problem is that with multiple deck headlines, often the interlinear space is kerned, and the ascending letters on lower lines commit acts of gross indecency on descending letters in the line above.

It's when letters merge, as in the bottom line of Figure 26, that the reader cries, "Stop, enough!"

Not one reader in the study indicated that headlines in which the letters merged were easy to read. The comprehension level was zero.

Figure 26

Letterspacing affects legibility.

Letterspacing affects legibility.

Letterspacing affects legibility.

Letterspacing affects legibility.

Letterspacing affects legibility.

Kerning, from natural setting (middle)
to loose (top) and tight (bottom), equivalent
to variations from one to four units.
The typeface is Times New Roman.

As kerning units vary between phototypesetters, it could be that three units in one system could parallel four in another. The eyes should be the best guide.

It's important also to consider the medium on which the work is to be printed. A headline kerned three units may look fine on a photomechanical transfer, but if it is to be printed on newsprint by a coldset press, ink absorption could cause the letters to bleed into one another. A classic example of this appeared in a Sydney suburban newspaper. The heading should have read, "Jogging burns excess energy."

Regrettably, the letters *r* and *n* in the word *burns* merged. The result should be obvious.

Table 6 (next page) shows the relative legibility of headlines set natural and kerned. The figures indicate the positive response as a percentage of the total reader sample.

The conclusion must be that capital letter headlines are less legible than lower case headlines.

There seems little to choose between serif and sans serif, or between modern and old style roman, or between roman and italic.

It is also clear that ornamental, script, cursive, and black letter faces should be avoided if the headline is designed to be understood. (Examples appear in Figure 27 on page 75.)

It is difficult to understand why designers should be so entranced by kerning, particularly in its extreme use.

Table 6

Times Roman

	Lower case	Capitals
Natural	93%	68%
Kerned one unit	92%	66%
Kerned two units	67%	53%
Kerned three units	44%	41%
Kerned four units	0%	0%

Helvetica Bold

	Lower case	Capitals
Natural	92%	55%
Kerned one unit	93%	56%
Kerned two units	79%	48%
Kerned three units	74%	44%
Kerned four units	0%	0%

Figure 27

An ornamental typeface (Bernhard Fashion).

A script typeface (Forte).

A cursive typeface (Bernhard Tango).

A black letter typeface (Old English).

Avoid decorative typefaces like these
if you want your headline to be understood.

Conclusions

¶ *There is little difference in legibility between headlines set in*
serif and sans serif typefaces, or between roman and italic.

¶ *Headlines set in capital letters are significantly less legible*
than those set in lower case.

¶ *Kerning headline type may undermine legibility. Not one*
reader in the study indicated that headlines in which the
letters merged were easy to read.

SIX

Any Color
as Long as It's Black

CONSIDER THIS PAGE. It looks very much like any other page, with its ordinary black type printed on ordinary white paper.

Color the type blue, and imagine how much more attractive the page might become to the reader's eye. If you were to show potential readers the two pages together, the chances are that eight out of 10 would find the blue printed page more attractive than the black one, and that nine out of 10 would probably describe the black page as boring.

But ask those people now to read the two pages, and we're in a different ball game.

The chances now are that seven out of 10 who read the black text would display comprehension sound enough to enable them to digest the text and act on any message it contains, but of those who attempted to read the visually more attractive colored text, only one out of 10 would display good comprehension.

Not a very attractive result, you may agree, particularly if the aim of the text is to sell something.

Spot color can do wonders for advertising revenue. This is unassailable. U.S. research tells us about one advertiser who paid a premium of 70 per cent for spot color and drew nearly 400 per cent more sales. Spot color generally adds to the cost of an advertisement by 20 per cent or more, but the advertisement is noted by 63 percent more people and results in 64 per cent more sales.

What the research doesn't tell us is how the color was used. One can understand a positive impact when spot color is used on logotypes and ideograms such as BP, Shell, Ford, the Mitsubishi diamonds, Coke, and so on, but what about headlines? Or the text?

What's the effect on the reader if the color is used as part or all of the message, instead of as an ancillary?

Color imparts a feeling of excitement, and most certainly is a magnet for the eyes.

The purpose of these tests was to determine if that magnet might impart a negative influence—that is, whether color used in headlines or text might impede comprehension.

Colored headlines

Most frequent use of color in headlines is high chroma color, such as the process colors, cyan and magenta.

Other high chroma colors, such as hot red, bright green and orange are becoming more and more common in newspapers and magazines as the range of press color availability increases.

Tests were made of both high chroma and low chroma colors.

In the first tests, colors used were magenta (process red), cyan (process blue), hot red (100 parts magenta, 100 yellow), hot orange (100 yellow, 40 magenta), and lime green (100 yellow, 40 cyan).

Results applying to each individual color were so similar as to enable a general conclusion to be drawn about high chroma color.

The test procedure was identical to previous ones, with the obvious exception that color headlines were substituted for black headlines.

This aspect of the program attracted considerable comment from readers:

» 61 per cent of all readers said they found high chroma colors most attractive, drawing their attention quickly to the text.

» 47 per cent said they then found the headings hard to read.

» 64 per cent said they found the color intruding while they were trying to read the text.

» 12 per cent said they felt the same effect as an obtrusive light, or an over-bright color television picture, distracting the eyes.

» 10 per cent found the high chroma colors intense and tending to cause eye-tiredness.

The stock used for this series of tests was, as with all tests, non-reflective.

A small number of readers (two per cent) indicated afterwards that, anxious to continue the test to the best of their ability, they folded the pages over to mask the colored headlines and to enable them to concentrate better. An inspection of retrieved papers showed this to be the case.

The tests for low chroma colors were done in an identical manner.

The low chroma colors chosen were deep blue (100 parts cyan, 50 black), dark emerald (100 yellow, 100 cyan, 40 black), purple (100 cyan, 100 magenta), and plum red (100 magenta, 60 black). Comments made on these tests implied that the colored headlines didn't have the same magnetic quality that the high chroma colors had.

However, there was a degree of attraction, in both positive and negative aspects. The good comprehension levels in this test were three times as high as those for high chroma colors, but less than 80 per cent of those for black headings. Results follow as Table 7.

Table 7

| | Comprehension Level | | |
	Good	Fair	Poor
Layout with black headlines	67%	19%	14%
Layout using high chroma color headlines	17%	18%	65%
Layout using low chroma color headlines	52%	28%	20%

Obviously, there's a paradox. To be valuable as an eye-catching device, a colored headline needs to be in a vibrant color, which tends to disqualify it as a means of communication.

The study showed that the darker the headline, the greater the comprehension level. This poses the question, why not black? Ink doesn't come any darker!

Comments made by readers show that the use of process colors in headlines is dangerous. Although the results indicated greater comprehension levels than, say, layouts set in sans serif body type, the spot color headlines in high chroma showed a greater potential to antagonize some readers.

This is not a recommendation that a ban be placed on headline spot color. Used judiciously and sparingly, color can be a most compelling and useful heading feature. But great care should be taken that the color doesn't get in the way of the message.

Colored text

In the past five years, the use of colored text, and text printed on colored tints, has proliferated, without, as it were, benefit of clergy.

Little or no research exists, either to support or condemn the practice.

Miles Tinker, with his *Legibility of Print* (Iowa State University Press, 1963), stands almost in isolation. His view is that there should be at least 70 per cent differential between text and background—that is, if the text is printed solid, then the background *should be no more than 30 per cent tint.*

Figure 28

This text is printed in black on a 30% tint of black. Miles Tinker says this 70% contrast is sufficient to ensure legibility. Not everyone agrees.

This text is printed in the grayscale equivalent of cyan on a 10% tint of cyan. Miles Tinker says this 70% contrast is sufficient to ensure legibility. Not everyone agrees.

The text above is printed 100% black on 30% black (top), and the grayscale equivalents of 100% cyan on 30% cyan (bottom).

Obviously, this might be held to apply for black, or dark colors such as deep purple, navy blue, and dark brown. But what about cyan or magenta, which are much lighter to start with? What effect does printing text in cyan on a 30 per cent cyan tint have on the reader? (For a hint, see Figure 28 above.)

In an attempt to remedy this apparent research deficiency, tests were run using text printed in black and in several colors on white paper; in black and in several colors on tinted paper; in black on shades of gray; in reverse, using black and color; and in bold type, contrasted with the normal medium density type used in advertising and newspaper editorial matter for body text.

For the color text studies, articles presented to the readers were set in 10 point Times Roman type over 12 points (5 cm) to a depth of 18 cm, three columns to a page. Each article had a single line heading set in 36 point Univers bold lower case, printed black, and above the three columns of text.

The layout and type employed were in a format which previous research had shown offers minimal distraction for the reader, thus enabling the text matter in its varied hues to stand or fall solely on the merits of those hues.

All results given are expressed in percentages of the total sample.

Articles were presented to readers in six forms: in black; in PMS (Pantone Matching System) 259, a deep purple; in PMS 286, French blue; in PMS 399, a muted color resembling olive green; and in two high intensity colors, warm red and process blue (cyan), all on white paper.

When the text was printed black, the comprehension levels were similar to those obtained in previous tests conducted on similarly designed material.

The good comprehension level was 70 per cent, fair comprehension 19 per cent, and poor comprehension 11 per cent.

There is probably nothing the typographer can do to ensure a 100 per cent level of good comprehension on anything more complex than today's page of the desk calendar. It's probably true to say that there are readers who would overlook or misunderstand an article documenting the Second Coming!

The responses to text printed in colors showed a considerably lower level of good comprehension than in the tests for black printed on white.

Initially, tests were conducted separately on matte and gloss paper, it being considered possible that what was good on matte might be even better on gloss, or that glossy paper might, through its reflective quality, be an inferior reading medium.

However, results showed little variation in good comprehension levels. During the tests it was noticed that when readers experienced discomfort because of reflection from glossy paper, they altered their positions, or the position of the paper, to minimize this problem.

Tests of matte versus gloss were conducted with text printed in black; in medium intensity color; and in high intensity color. In each instance, results were within two per cent of each other.

As this variation was statistically insignificant, the tests were abandoned, and all further tests conducted on uncoated stock.

At the conclusion of each test on colored text, participants were asked to comment on the presentation of each paper. A summary of comments, collected for anecdotal purposes, is:

» 76 per cent said they found text printed in high intensity colors difficult to read. The color tended to break concentration, they said, and many found they lost their place and had to recapitulate. The brightness of the color appeared to cause lines to merge, making reading difficult.

» There was no variation in the extent of this effect between text set in process blue and warm red.

» An analysis of questions and answers showed that few readers retained any comprehension of the text printed in bright colors beyond the first few paragraphs.

» 41 per cent of readers indicated there was insufficient contrast between brightly colored text and the paper background, despite the intensity of the color.

» 68 per cent indicated the same effect when the text was printed in olive green (PMS 399).

» On being shown pages printed in black and in cyan, 90 per cent said they found the black page boring when compared with the blue printed page.

» And 81 per cent said they would prefer to read the colored page because it was more attractive. The dire consequences of accepting this view follow in Table 8.

» 63 per cent said the medium intensity color, PMS 286, provided concentration problems. Again, lines of type appeared to merge. This phenomenon occurred less with the low intensity color (deep purple) and hardly at all with black.

Table 8

	Comprehension Level		
	Good	Fair	Poor
Text printed in black	70%	19%	11%
Low intensity color (deep purple, PMS 259)	51%	13%	36%
Medium intensity color (French blue, PMS 286)	29%	22%	49%
Muted color (olive green, PMS 399)	10%	13%	77%
High intensity color (cyan or warm red)	10%	9%	81%

» All of those (36 per cent of the sample) who exhibited poor comprehension of the text printed deep purple said they believed their concentration suffered simply because they were aware the text wasn't printed black.

» Every reader said he or she would prefer to read text printed in black.

Text on tinted backgrounds

A second series of tests, using identical methodology, probed the comprehensibility of text on tinted backgrounds.

Six separate series of tests were conducted, using black on process blue tints, PMS 259 on its tints, PMS 286 on its tints, process blue on its tints, black on tints of olive green (PMS 399), and PMS 399 on its tints.

Readers were given samples with text printed on tints of 10 per cent of the base color, and increased in strength in increments of 10 percent.

Again, readers were invited to comment on the presentation of the text. More than half of those who responded to the invitation made a comment with an interesting marketing application: at low strength tint, the tint seemed to soften the harshness of the white paper (this supposed harshness had not been mentioned before, nor was it afterwards). The softening effect of the tinted background, they said, made reading easier. At high strength, the tint intruded and made reading more difficult.

Figure 29

Text printed in black on the equivalent of 10% cyan.

Text printed in black on the equivalent of 20% cyan.

Text printed in black on the equivalent of 30% cyan.

Text printed in black on the equivalent of 40% cyan.

Text printed in black on the grayscale equivalents of cyan at 10%, 20%, 30%, and 40% intensity.

However, while results of the test supported the latter view, they did not confirm the former.

The results of the tint tests are to be found on the following pages in Tables 9 through 14.

Table 9

Black on Cyan Tints

	Comprehension Level		
	Good	Fair	Poor
Black on 10% tint	68%	24%	8%
Black on 20% tint	56%	21%	23%
Black on 30% tint	38%	19%	43%
Black on 40% tint	22%	12%	66%

This test was discontinued when the combined results for good and fair comprehension failed to reach 50 percent of the total.

Table 10

PMS 259 on Its Tints

	Comprehension Level		
	Good	Fair	Poor
PMS 259 on 10% tint	50%	14%	36%
PMS 259 on 20% tint	32%	10%	58%

This test was discontinued when the combined results for good and fair comprehension failed to reach 50 percent of the total.

Table 11

PMS 286 on Its Tints

	Comprehension Level		
	Good	Fair	Poor
PMS 286 on 10% tint	27%	16%	57%
PMS 286 on 20% tint	12%	10%	78%

This test was discontinued because the combined results for good and fair comprehension failed to reach 50 percent of the total.

Table 12

Cyan on Its Tints

	Comprehension Level		
	Good	Fair	Poor
Cyan on 10% tint	6%	7%	87%
Cyan on 20% tint	0%	2%	98%

This test was discontinued because the combined results for good and fair comprehension failed to reach 50 percent of the total.

Table 13

Black on PMS 399 Tints

	Comprehension Level		
	Good	Fair	Poor
Black on 10% PMS 399 tint	68%	26%	6%
Black on 20% PMS 399 tint	53%	21%	26%
Black on 30% PMS 399 tint	32%	19%	49%
Black on 40% PMS 399 tint	22%	13%	65%

This test was discontinued when the combined results for good and fair comprehension failed to reach 50 percent of the total.

Table 14

PMS 399 on Its Tints

	Comprehension Level		
	Good	Fair	Poor
PMS 399 on 10% tint	8%	8%	84%
PMS 399 on 20% tint	2%	6%	92%
PMS 399 on 30% tint	0%	3%	97%

This test was discontinued because the combined results for good and fair comprehension failed to reach 50 percent of the total.

In these tests of lighter or more intensive color on tints, participants displayed their strongest reactions to any aspect of the program.

In the test of cyan on a 10 per cent tint of cyan, 42 per cent of readers indicated they had not attempted to continue reading seriously after a few paragraphs.

When the tint was increased to 20 per cent, the percentage of "conscientious objectors" rose to 53 per cent.

This declared stance was supported by an analysis of the results. For example, in the tests with cyan on a 20 per cent cyan tint, 99 per cent of correct answers related to questions in the first leg of text, indicating a reluctance or inability to digest the entire article. Yet the same articles, presented in black to control groups, offered no difficulties.

The reasons given by the readers were the apparent brightness of the color, and the difficulty readers had in distinguishing text from background. The brightness element applied also during tests using PMS 286.

The same results were apparent in the test of PMS 399 on tints of the same color, but brightness wasn't a problem with this test. The principal reason given was the similarity in color of text and ground.

Readers said they found the test using PMS 259 on its 10 per cent tint pleasant to the eyes, but many said they were conscious of the presence of color, which may have affected concentration.

Prior to the tests, readers were simultaneously shown printed pages in all three forms (black on white, black on tint, and color on tint) and asked to make subjective judgments on their relative attractiveness.

Results of this test contrasted markedly with those of an earlier experiment into the relative attractiveness of black and colored text, cited above.

In the test we are presently considering, the results are recorded in Table 15.

Table 15

	"Most Attractive"
Black text	8%
Black text on 10% cyan	88%
Cyan on 10% cyan	4%
Black text	17%
Black text on 10% olive green	83%
Olive green on 10% olive green	0%

From this assessment it would appear that black text printed on light tint is an attractive marketing proposition, as well as having high comprehensibility.

It would also appear that not only are colors on their tints extremely difficult to comprehend, they are also unattractive to the reader, except when the color is of low intensity and dark.

Figure 30

Text printed in black on white.

Text printed in black on 10% gray.

Text printed in black on 20% gray.

Text printed in black on 30% gray.

Text printed on white and on shades of gray.

There is obviously a cost factor in printing a second color. But to judge by the readers' assessments and the objective comprehension levels recorded in this study, there must also be a considerable marketing benefit in printing black on a tint.

By the same criteria, there must also be a considerable cost disadvantage in printing in one color—if that color is not black.

Black on not so black

A frequently used variation on the use of black on tinted grounds is to print black text on shades of gray.

This is generally used when only one color is available in an attempt to present associated material in a manner different from that used for the main text. The same methodology was used to test the comprehensibility of this element, and the results are shown in Table 16 (opposite page).

One significant comment, made frequently as the shade strength increased beyond 10 per cent, was that readers were experiencing more difficulty discerning the words. It was like trying to read a newspaper in poor light.

Table 16

	Comprehension Level		
	Good	Fair	Poor
Black on white	70%	19%	11%
Black on 10% black	63%	22%	15%
Black on 20% black	33%	18%	49%
Black on 30% black	3%	10%	87%

Into reverse

David Ogilvy says that advertising copy should never be set in reverse, nor over gray or colored tint. He says the old school "believed these devices forced people to read the copy; we now know that they make reading physically impossible."

The results of tests on text set in black on light color tints oppose his view. The tests on black text set on shades of gray are more on his side, and the tests on text printed in reverse on black or dark colors support his view to the hilt.

Participants in these tests of text printed in reverse reported a form of light vibration, similar to, but worse than, that encountered when text was printed in high intensity colors. This vibration seemed to make the lines of type move and merge into one another. Eighty per cent reported this phenomenon. The results are reported in Table 17.

Table 17

| | Comprehension Level | | |
	Good	Fair	Poor
Text printed black on white	70%	19%	11%
Text printed white on black	0%	12%	88%
Text printed white on PMS 259	2%	16%	82%
Text printed white on PMS 286	0%	4%	96%

There is a school of thought which agrees that reversing can be fraught with danger, but only if serif type is used. The argument is that the fine strokes and serifs disappear when the material is reversed.

To test this, similar articles were prepared set in 10 point Univers, with all other dimensions being identical to the remainder of the test papers.

With the text printed black, comprehension levels were comparable with those recorded in the tests of sans serif versus serif body matter. Good comprehension was 14 per cent, fair comprehension 25 per cent, and poor comprehension 61 per cent.

With the text reversed, comprehensibility dropped considerably. Good comprehension dropped to 4 per cent, and fair comprehension to 13 per cent. Poor comprehension rose to 83 per cent.

It could be said that the depreciation in comprehensibility appears to be proportionately less when the type is set in sans serif—but this argument only holds water if a level of good comprehension of less than five per cent is considered acceptable.

Bold and bad

A final series of tests was conducted with text printed in bold type. This generally is used as a means of separating a subsidiary article from a major one, or to break up the monotony of an article.

It certainly has those effects: it also has the effect of ensuring that the subsidiary article is harder to read. Readers in this test complained of fatigue, similar to that experienced when text was printed in high or medium intensity colors.

The bold text, occupying more of the letter space allocated to it than normal roman type, seemed to some readers to be cramped.

To others it seemed to set up a halo effect, carrying the outline of letters into adjoining letters and onto the lines above and below.

The results are summarized below in Table 18.

Figure 31

An ad such as this that makes prominent use of
white or colored text on black background
risks losing readers in droves.

Table 18

| | Comprehension Level | | |
	Good	Fair	Poor
Text printed in Times Roman	70%	19%	11%
Text printed in Times Roman Bold	30%	20%	50%

It's impossible to avoid the fact that comprehensibility of colored text increases as the color gets closer to black.

So why not use black, and employ color where it's best suited, as a complement to the message?

We should consider carefully Edmund Arnold's advice: "Start with good typography—the kind that best suits the reader—and use color to reinforce the communication."

Conclusions

¶ *The darker the headline, the greater the comprehension level. Black headlines were well understood by nearly four times as many readers as brightly colored headlines.*

¶ *Text must be printed in black. Even copy set in deep colors was substantially more difficult for readers to understand. Seven times as many participants in the study demonstrated good comprehension when text was black as opposed to either muted or high intensity colors.*

¶ *Black text printed on light tint is an attractive marketing proposition, as well as having high comprehensibility.*

¶ *Readers find tinted backgrounds attractive.*

¶ *When black text is printed on a gray background, readers experience difficulties discerning the words when the shade strength is increased beyond 10 per cent.*

¶ *Printing text in white on a black or colored background makes it virtually impossible for readers to understand. This is true whether the text is set in serif or sans serif type.*

¶ *Printing text in boldface type undermines reading comprehension. Fewer than half the number of readers will easily understand the message.*

§ *SEVEN*

Is Italic Body Type as Black as It's Painted?

EDITORS THROUGHOUT THE WESTERN WORLD
have clung to the proposition that italic body type is illegible
as though it were Holy Writ. There is, however, no reason
why this should be true. Italic letters do not lack any of the
characteristics that distinguish their roman counterparts.
(Sans serif body types have been discarded.)

Figure 32

It's difficult to understand how italic type has acquired such an unsavory reputation. Conventional wisdom notwithstanding, italic body text poses no difficulties for readers.

It's difficult to understand how italic type has acquired such an unsavory reputation. Conventional wisdom notwithstanding, italic body text poses no difficulties for readers.

One paragraph set in 15 point Goudy OldStyle,
first in italics, then in roman.

Serif italics have the same thick and thin strokes, the same x-height of their vertical fellows, and—possibly a virtue—they slope in the direction of reading and of normal handwriting.

True, some italic faces have elaborate swashes on some letters. This study was confined to those faces with minimal elaboration to the italic version of the face.

What then, has brought italic body type into such disrepute? It is difficult to see.

It is not the intention to advocate widespread use of italic type as body matter—merely to act as devil's advocate for a style of type which this analysis shows to be wrongly castigated.

The procedure was identical to that for other tests. The body types used were Corona Light roman and Corona Light italic, eight on nine point.

Readers' comments indicated that while italic type caused an initial reaction, because it was unusual in such volume, it caused no difficulty for the reader.

Table 19 shows the comprehension level of italic body type:

Table 19

	Comprehension Level		
	Good	Fair	Poor
Layout using Corona roman text	67%	19%	14%
Layout using Corona italic text	65%	19%	16%

Conclusion

¶ *Italic body type causes no more difficulty for readers than roman body type.*

EIGHT

Ragged Right or Left, or Justified?

RAGGED SETTING ON THE RIGHT was popularized by the designer Eric Gill in 1930 to eliminate the need—in book setting—for uneven spacings to fill out lines. There's some logic in this, even though the impact on the reader of the unesthetic spacing is questionable.

Figure 33

Ragged setting on the right was popularized by the designer Eric Gill in 1930 to eliminate the need—in book setting—for uneven spacings to fill out lines. There's some logic in this, even though the impact on the reader of the unesthetic spacing may be questionable. But there's very little logic in ragged right's sinister offspring, ragged left setting.

Ragged setting on the right was popularized by the designer Eric Gill in 1930 to eliminate the need—in book setting—for uneven spacings to fill out lines. There's some logic in this, even though the impact on the reader of the unesthetic spacing may be questionable. But there's very little logic in ragged right's sinister offspring, ragged left setting.

In ragged right setting (top), reading rhythm is interrupted. In ragged left body text (bottom), there is no Axis of Orientation.

But there's little logic in ragged right's sinister offspring, ragged left setting, as shown in Figure 33 (opposite).There are those who argue that for legibility all body type must be justified completely.

Some accept type that is unjustified or ragged at the right, as shown in Figure 33, and some magazine and advertising designers who strive for effect rather than com- munication occasionally set body matter ragged left.

Many type practitioners will allow ragged right setting yet steadfastly oppose ragged left. Those who accept ragged left setting usually accept both forms.

To test this element, papers were presented with totally justified setting, ragged right, and ragged left. Setting had to be modified slightly to accommodate the additional space required for ragged setting; the results apply to complete pages set ragged. The findings may not be appropriate to small amounts of ragged setting, as are shown in Figure 33.

Type used was Corona roman eight point on 8.5 point body, and the layout was identical to those used in tests on page design (Figure 9).

Comprehension levels are shown on the next page in Table 20.

The comprehension level—or lack thereof—of ragged left setting was similar to that for sans serif body type, yet paradoxically many designers who would never use ragged left setting have no qualms about ordering considerable volumes of setting in sans serif type.

Table 20

	Comprehension Level		
	Good	Fair	Poor
Layout with totally justified setting	67%	19%	14%
Layout with ragged right setting	38%	22%	40%
Layout with ragged left setting	10%	18%	72%

It would be interesting if a future researcher were to quantify the comprehensibility of sans serif type set ragged left, as is seen frequently in some magazines and in display advertising.

Conclusion

¶ *Ragged setting should be avoided if comprehensibility is to be maintained. Almost twice as many readers understand totally justified text than text set ragged right. Nearly seven times as many show good comprehension of justified compared to ragged left.*

§ *NINE*

The Big Squeeze

Back in the good old days of hot metal, when everything typographic was ordered and uncomplicated, type came in four basic widths—expanded, natural, condensed, and extra condensed.

But now, with digitized typesetting, literally anything goes. Type can be expanded, condensed, stretched, or squeezed to suit the designer's or typesetter's imagination—or possibly to try the reader's patience.

Figure 34

Any garden-variety desktop publishing system can work
wonders with type—but that's not always advisable.

The typesetter can make a headline fit around corners, squeeze it into half its original length, or italicize or backslant until the letters fall over.

Anything can be done to bolster the designer's genius, or perhaps to coddle the headline writer for an inability to write a headline that fits. But should technology serve only the designer and headline writer, or should it also serve the reader? Are we, by distorting type, discomfiting readers to such an extent that they will retaliate by the only means open to them—by refusing to read our message?

If this danger is real, how far down the primrose path can we go before our use of the technology available to us becomes counterproductive?

To find answers to some of these questions, a further research program with a sample of 500 was conducted in Sydney in 1986.

The findings were:

1. The point at which headlines, when condensed, become difficult to read appears to be at 70 per cent of natural width. About 39 per cent of the sample indicated this point, and a further 14 per cent indicated the threshold at three per cent above or below this width. This result applied to all styles shown to members of the sample.

2. The point of condensing at which headlines were deemed easiest to read was at 90 per cent of natural setting. About 40 per cent of the sample indicated this,

with a similar percentage nominating a width three percent above or below the 90 per cent width.

3. The style of headline setting deemed easiest to read was lower case condensed to 90 per cent of natural width, with no difference noted between sans serif and serif headlines. Where a choice of type was offered, all participants deemed lower case easier to read than capitals.

Conclusion

¶   *Slightly condensing headline type makes it easier to read. Settings between 70 per cent and 90 per cent of natural width appear to be optimal.*

TEN

Out, Damned Spot!

MANY ADVERTISING TYPOGRAPHERS place a period at the end of their headings. No newspaper typographers do. (See the sample advertisement in Figure 35 on the next page.)

The thinking is that editorial headlines in newspapers and magazines rarely form sentences and therefore don't need periods, but advertising headlines frequently form sentences and therefore require periods.

Figure 35

How to choose a charity to invest with.

Investing with a charity could give you a greater return on your money than investing yourself. But choosing the right charity to invest with is an important financial decision. You want smart investors who are experienced in the field of financial and retirement planning. You want a variety of financial products to choose from. And you want a stable organization with a history of putting money aside, keeping it and making it grow for people like you and the community whose needs it serves.

UJA-Federation of New York.
$370 Million in assets. And an unbeatable expert staff to help everyone from small investors to major philanthropists.

If it's financial security you're looking for, you can rest assured with UJA-Federation of New York. We've been providing charitable services to Israel and the Jewish community for 75 years. And we keep on going.

Whether you're simply looking to get a better return on a $10,000 investment or you're looking to hand-tailor a complex charitable program, we've got some of the best people to work with you and your own professional advisors. We develop strategy and plan and execute a wide variety of financial programs. Over 50 estate and financial professionals, both on staff and volunteer, including lawyers, accountants, tax specialists and financial planners help us maintain an unmatched pooled resource of counselling, up-to-date information and accounting and legal advice. Some of our staff are recognized experts in the field. And our advice is free.

What we always look for is a stable, reasonable, better than conservative return that often beats the current yield on your assets. If you invest with us, we're always aware that ultimately you're leaving us something in the future. We therefore owe you something today. And that's a solid return, a lot of security and a minimum of risk.

Life Income Plans.
How we help you while you help us.

If your personal financial goal is significant tax reduction or increased income, one of our life income plans could be right for you.

Our Charitable Remainder Trust pays you either an annuity (a set amount each year based on the initial principal you give us) or a fixed percentage of the principal re-valued each year. We keep paying you for your entire lifetime or up to 20 years, whichever you choose. After that, the remaining principal goes to UJA-Federation of New York to be used for the things that are important to you.

Charitable Gift Annuity of $10,000.

AGE	RATE	EQUIVALENT* ANNUAL RATE
65	7.3%	8.4% ($ 840)
70	7.8%	9.1% ($ 910)
75	8.5%	10.0% ($1,000)
80	9.6%	11.6% ($1,160)
85	10.9%	13.4% ($1,340)
90	12.0%	15.1% ($1,510)

*Net rate after tax savings from charitable deduction (assumes combined federal and state income tax rate of 35%)

For people under the age of 65, the Charitable Gift Annuity can be used for retirement planning as well. The annual annuity payments begin at age 65.

Our Charitable Gift Annuity offers added tax benefits. By purchasing a fixed annuity from us outright you are making partially tax deductible contributions. You therefore receive both income benefits and tax deductible benefits. This makes it a financial plan perfect for both retirees and for people planning their retirement. And we receive your contributions and put them to work for charity.

You pick the financial product. You pick the charity.

We've got lots of ways for you to invest and all let you meet your personal financial goals while really making a difference in the world. Our programs include life income plans like Charitable Remainder Trusts and Gift Annuities, tax-wise gifts of real estate and business interests, creative uses of personal property like art and collectibles, unique alternatives to private foundations and more. We also have special plans for protecting your IRA or other retirement plans from tax reduction. And you can designate your philanthropy to UJA-Federation of New York or to any of our 130 human and social service agencies in the Greater New York area or in Israel.

You can choose to let your money help needy children, the aged, disabled individuals. You can provide scholarships or resettle Soviet Jews. Or you can earmark your money for programs in Israel. Whatever you choose, you can rest assured that at UJA-Federation of New York we can find the right financial program for you. And the right cause.

Financial Stability and Philanthropy.
Nobody puts the two together better than we do.

You demand some financial stability. And you recognize that you've reached a time in your life when you want to give something back. The Department of Planned Giving and Endowments of UJA-Federation of New York lets you do both efficiently, profitably and with a minimum of risk.

To find out how you can meet your financial goals and help support a wide variety of charities, make an appointment to see one of our experts today. It could make a big difference in your future. And in ours.

Department of Planned Giving and Endowments
UJA-Federation of New York
130 East 59th Street, New York, NY 10022
NYTM594

For more information or to arrange a free confidential consultation with no obligation, clip this coupon or call Neal Myerberg at 212-836-1811 today.

☐ Please call me. I'd like to set up an appointment to meet one of your planned giving experts.
☐ Please send me more information about:
☐ Charitable Gift Annuities ☐ Current Payments ☐ Deferred Payments
☐ Charitable Remainder Trusts ☐ Gifts of Real Estate ☐ Private Foundation Alternatives
☐ Gifts of Personal Property ☐ Protecting Private or Company Retirement Plans
☐ Other _____

Name _____
Address _____
City _____ State _____ Zip _____
Age (optional) _____ Tel _____ Best time to call _____

UJA-FEDERATION OF NEW YORK
We help 4.5 million people a year. One at a time.

THE NEW YORK TIMES MAGAZINE / JUNE 19, 1994 19

A period at the end of a headline
could bring the reader to a full stop.

To find whether the period has an effect on readers' comprehension, and if that effect is significant, a project was conducted in Sydney between December 1986 and March 1987, at the request of David Ogilvy.

Magazine pages were created in the Ayer No. 1 format: a slightly less than half-page horizontal illustration, with a headline below it, and the text below again. (See Figure 36 on the next page.) Four different pages were printed, with each design being in two formats—one with the headline ending with a period, the other without.

The content of two of the designs was editorial, with a tourism theme, and the content of the other two was advertising, with a motoring theme. One was an adaptation of the classic Ogilvy Rolls-Royce advertisement.

There were no significant differences between the individual designs in levels of comprehension. There were, however, differences in comprehension between the headlines ending in periods and those in editorial style. See Table 21 (page 119) for the results of this comparison.

Figure 36

The headline appears under the illustration

Text follows neatly below the headline in the Ayer No. 1 format. As we learned earlier, this simple format helps the reader. It respects reading gravity. Text follows neatly below the headline in the Ayer No. 1 format. As we learned earlier, this simple format helps the reader. It respects reading gravity. Text follows neatly below the headline in the Ayer No. 1 format. As we learned earlier, this simple format helps the reader. It respects reading gravity. Text follows neatly below the headline in the Ayer No. 1 format. As we learned earlier, this simple format helps the reader. It respects reading gravity. Text follows neatly below the headline in the Ayer No. 1 format. As we learned earlier, this simple format helps the reader. It respects reading gravity. Text follows neatly below the headline in the Ayer No. 1 format. As we learned earlier, this simple format helps the reader. It respects reading gravity. Text follows neatly below the headline in the Ayer No. 1 format. As we learned earlier, this simple format helps the reader. It respects reading gravity. Text follows neatly below the headline in the Ayer No. 1 format. As we learned earlier, this simple format helps the reader. It

respects reading gravity. Text follows neatly below the headline in the Ayer No. 1 format. As we learned earlier, this simple format helps the reader. It respects reading gravity. Text follows neatly below the headline in the Ayer No. 1 format. As we learned earlier, this simple format helps the reader. It respects reading gravity. Text follows neatly below the headline in the Ayer No. 1 format. As we learned earlier, this simple format helps the reader. It respects reading gravity. Text follows neatly below the headline in the Ayer No. 1 format. As we learned earlier, this simple format helps the reader. It respects reading gravity. Text follows neatly below the headline in the Ayer No. 1 format. As we learned earlier, this simple format helps the reader. It respects reading gravity. Text follows neatly below the headline in the Ayer No. 1 format. As we learned earlier, this simple format helps the reader. It respects reading gravity. Text follows neatly below the headline in the Ayer No. 1 format. As we learned earlier, this simple format

helps the reader. It respects reading gravity. Text follows neatly below the headline in the Ayer No. 1 format. As we learned earlier, this simple format helps the reader. It respects reading gravity. Text follows neatly below the headline in the Ayer No. 1 format. As we learned earlier, this simple format helps the reader. It respects reading gravity. Text follows neatly below the headline in the Ayer No. 1 format. As we learned earlier, this simple format helps the reader. It respects reading gravity. Text follows neatly below the headline in the Ayer No. 1 format. As we learned earlier, this simple format helps the reader. It respects reading gravity. Text follows neatly below the headline in the Ayer No. 1 format. As we learned earlier, this simple format helps the reader. It respects reading gravity. Text follows neatly below the headline in the Ayer No. 1 format. As we learned earlier, this simple format helps the reader. It respects reading gravity. Text follows neatly below the headline in the Ayer No. 1 format. As we learned earlier,

The Ayer No. 1 format.

Table 21

	Comprehension Level		
	Good	Fair	Poor
Headline without a period	71%	19%	10%
Headline with a period	58%	22%	20%

After the project was completed, the members of the sample were questioned on their reactions to the material. Those who read the headlines with periods were conscious of the punctuation mark and commented on it.

Twenty-two per cent of the total sample said they realized they were reading an advertisement when they came to the period, even though they were not at that point aware of the content.

Ten per cent of the sample indicated this discovery diminished their intention to concentrate on reading the material.

Twelve per cent of the sample indicated they found the use of the periods unnatural and wondered why they had been used. Six per cent of the sample said the period indicated to them that there was no need to read any more of the message. All that needed to be said had been said.

The conclusion is that the use of periods at the end of headlines in advertisements with a considerable amount (50%) of reading matter may have a detrimental effect on readers' comprehension. In the project, 13 per cent fewer readers displayed good comprehension when periods were used.

Reasons for this were:

» The period tends to pull some readers up with a jerk and indicate to them there is no need to read on.

» The full stop is, to some readers, an indication that what follows is advertising material, and, in their minds, not as consequential as if it were editorial.

» Only two per cent of the sample were aware of the subtle distinction that editorial headlines rarely include verbs and that advertising headlines frequently do.

Note that the method used did not permit testing of advertisements which relied only on a headline without supporting text. Logically, the full stop in these circumstances would have little or no effect on comprehension.

Conclusion

¶ *Using periods at the end of headlines may have a detrimental effect on readers' comprehension.*

ELEVEN

Widows, Jumps, and Bastard Measure

THROUGHOUT THE PROGRAM, readers were asked to express opinions on minor typographical elements. We inquired whether widows (lines of type of less than full length at the head of a column) annoyed them. We sought their reactions when asked to jump from one page to another to continue an article.

We also questioned whether they found extremely narrow or extremely wide measure body type easy to read. And we sought to determine the value of subheads. Current newspapers and magazines were used to exemplify the elements being discussed.

The results were calculated, and are expressed here as percentages.

Design

»   61 per cent of readers said that jumps, where an article is continued on a later page, or on several later pages in successive jumps, were annoying.

»   66 per cent said they disliked pages which had large headlines with two or three paragraphs of copy, followed by an exhortation to jump to a later page. This was particularly disliked when the article was found to be inconsequential, such as an injury to a jockey's armpit, or merely a newspaper promotion stunt.

»   83 per cent said they usually disobeyed jumps. This may not concern advertising people—but what if their advertisement is on a jump page? It will need to be brilliant to be read!

»   39 per cent said that if they were convinced to jump to continue reading an article, they frequently discovered they had not returned to where they were originally reading.

»   67 per cent said they preferred illustrations to carry a description, such as a caption. The practice of some publications of describing an illustration in an accompanying article was frequently criticized.

» 81 per cent said they found special screening effects on illustrations such as mezzotype, circular line, and horizontal line to be annoying. Some said they thought the screens a device intended to disguise a poor illustration—or a printer's mistake!

» 77 per cent said they were annoyed by articles in which body type jumped over an illustration or pull quote, contrary to the natural flow of reading. The natural expectation was that once a barrier such as an illustration or pull quote was reached, the article would be continued at the head of the next leg of type.

The moral is clear: it's not difficult to annoy a reader, either by commission or omission. And the message is also clear: before the editor or designer inserts a typographical element, he or she should think hard about the effect it may have on the reader.

Headlines

» 57 per cent said they disliked "screamer" headlines, such as are used on the front pages of some popular tabloid newspapers and in some large display advertisements, because they had to hold the newspaper or magazine further than usual from the eyes to be able to read the type. The criterion for annoyance was the need to focus twice to read the entire content. (See Figure 37, next page.)

Figure 37

A magazine layout with headline type big enough to announce the Second Coming, and which forces the reader to focus twice–on the head and on the text.

» Multi-deck headlines were generally disliked. 56 per cent indicated they found headlines of more than four decks difficult to comprehend.

» 68 per cent said they became bored with long, wordy headlines. The comment was made frequently that there seemed to be nothing left to read after the headline. This, admittedly, is subjective—but the warning is there.

Body type

» 38 per cent of readers found body type set wider than 60 characters hard to read. A further 22 per cent indicated they probably wouldn't read wide measure body type even though they didn't find any difficulty reading it.

» 87 per cent said they found extremely narrow measure, such as less than 20 characters, hard to read.

» 78 per cent indicated they found subheads useful, particularly in long articles. None said they found subheads unattractive or intrusive.

None said they were offended by—or even were aware of—widows. (As the definition of a widow varies, we are considering here a short line which ends a paragraph, and which stands alone at the top of the adjoining column. In practice, the widow has the effect of forcing the reader to continue to the next column.) Apparently only printers and editors are offended!

Figure 38

Your equity offering is 20 minutes old and the bears think they smell breakfast.

You knew this wouldn't be easy.

The market's been turbulent. This morning's news from Europe sent interest rates up, the dollar down and the futures markets to discounts. So trading has been slack from the opening bell, and now the bargain hunters are trying to cut your price.

This is a crucial moment for you — and your investment bank. It's why you were so careful in selecting them.

They did their homework and won your business. Then they sat with you and built a strategy. Struck the right balance for your issue's size and price. Searched the world markets for the right core investors — pinpointing the ones who'd make long-term commitments.

They set up satellite presentations to analysts. Went on the road with you. Put all their firm's resources and disciplines to work for you. And came up with useful ideas all along the way.

But right now, none of that counts.

It's what they do in the next five minutes that will tell the story.

You know they'll stand firm. You chose these people because of their reputation — not just for having certain intellectual and financial capacities — but for knowing when and how to use them.

MORGAN STANLEY

Chicago   Frankfurt   Hong Kong   London   Los Angeles   Luxembourg   Madrid   Melbourne   Milan   New York   Paris   San Francisco   Seoul   Singapore   Taipei   Tokyo   Toronto   Zurich

This otherwise excellent layout deters readers with its wide measure body type.

Type & Layout

Only 7 per cent of readers said they found body matter set in capitals easy to read. Readers were shown text set in nine point Univers over 13 picas to a depth of 20 centimeters. A central section five centimeters deep was set in capitals, and readers were asked to indicate if they found this section easy to read. An overwhelming 93 per cent said no. They were then shown similar material set to the same dimensions in Corona Light, a serif face. The results were identical. When similar material was presented entirely in Univers lower case, 22 per cent said they found it easy to read. With Corona lower case 100 per cent said they found it easy to read.

Conclusions

¶ *Readers are easily annoyed. Most test subjects complained about special screening effects on illustrations; articles in which body type jumps over an illustration or pull quote; multi-deck headlines; long, wordy headlines; and jumps (which four out of five claimed to disobey).*

¶ *Readers prefer captions over descriptions in accompanying articles.*

¶ *Most readers find subheads useful, especially in longer articles.*

¶ *Both wide measure and narrow measure text are hard to read.*

¶ *Text set in capitals is difficult to read.*

TWELVE

Why They Don't Read Your Inserts

IN 1988 A MAJOR AUSTRALIAN ORGANIZATION decided to produce a leaflet to be inserted in newspapers and magazines. It called in an advertising agency and commissioned a one-color leaflet for a long print run. But somewhere along the track, between the creative spark and the reader, the wheels fell off.

The leaflet had a headline on the front, and two pages of text on the inside. When the leaflet was subjected to a readership research study, the level of poor comprehension was shown to be 62 per cent, with 29 per cent displaying fair comprehension, and only 9 per cent displaying good comprehension. What that means in effect is that only one reader in 10 had much idea of what the leaflet was about. And that figure was of those who actually took the trouble to read it.

Now in Figure 39 (opposite page) you may notice a couple of questionable typographic features.

First, the leaflet was set in sans serif type. A considerable body of research, including this study, shows that while sans serif may be clear-cut, modern, authoritative, decisive, sharp, and exciting—these are all creative department adjectives—it is notoriously difficult to read in continuous text.

Second, the leaflet was a headless wonder. David Ogilvy, who knows about these matters, rails against them, and Professor Siegfried Vögele, Dean of the Institute of Direct Marketing in Munich, has, with his eye-camera technique, shown them inadequate.

Vögele's eye-camera times and tracks the eye movements of readers when they come upon a printed spread.

Here's what he has found: When a potential reader comes upon a spread, the eyes alight at the top right corner, possibly because this is the first point exposed when a leaflet is opened or a newspaper or magazine page turned. From this point at the top right corner the eyes make a parabolic sweep to the left and then back and down to the right, sending messages to the brain when they make a fix on display elements. At the end of that sweep the brain makes

Figure 39

Australia's motorists will pay the Federal Government a whopping $6.5 billion in fuel taxes this year.

Last year, only personal income tax earned more revenue for the Federal Government.

Every time a driver stops at a petrol bowser, half the money he spends on petrol goes to the Government.

Which means petrol, a necessity, attracts a 150 percent tax. While "luxuries" such as jewellery, cosmetics and hi-fi equipment attract 30 percent tax.

Where does all the revenue from petrol tax go?

Not where it should. Less than 20 percent of this Federal tax is spent on Australia's roads.

After allowing for inflation, the amount the Federal Government is spending on roads is 25 percent less than it was three years ago.

Because roads require regular maintenance, State Road authorities are having to spend 60 percent of their available funds keeping them in reasonable shape.

However, this percentage is presently rising, leaving less each year for the development and extension of the nation's road network.

As a result, traffic in our major cities is grinding to a halt.

Vehicles spend up to one third of urban peak travel time standing still, wasting fuel.

Rough roads, both in the city and country, can increase fuel consumption by up to 20 percent and vehicle repair costs by 36 percent.

Poor roads also contribute to crashes, which last year cost the community $5,700 million.

Better roads save lives.

Replacing a two-lane road with a freeway, for instance, can reduce crashes by up to 85 percent.

Australians rely on their roads. Over 97 percent of passenger travel is on the nation's roads.

Nearly 83 percent of domestic tourist travel is by road, as is 43 percent of travel between capital cities by visiting international tourists.

Adding to the problem is the expectation that Australians will increase their use of the road network considerably over the next decade.

The number of cars and station wagons estimated to be using the roads by the end of the century will be 30 percent higher than today.

The amount of freight carried will increase by two-thirds.

You don't have to put up with bad roads.

If you think a greater share of the fuel taxes you pay should be spent on roads, talk to people about it.

Write to your newspaper. Tell your radio talkback show. Best of all, let your Federal MP or the Federal Minister for Transport and Communications know how you feel.

Tell them all that a greater share of the Federal petrol tax you pay should be spent on our roads.

A leaflet with no display.

a decision, based on the number or magnitude of the fixes made, whether there's enough incentive to read the spread. (See Figure 40, below.)

Figure 40

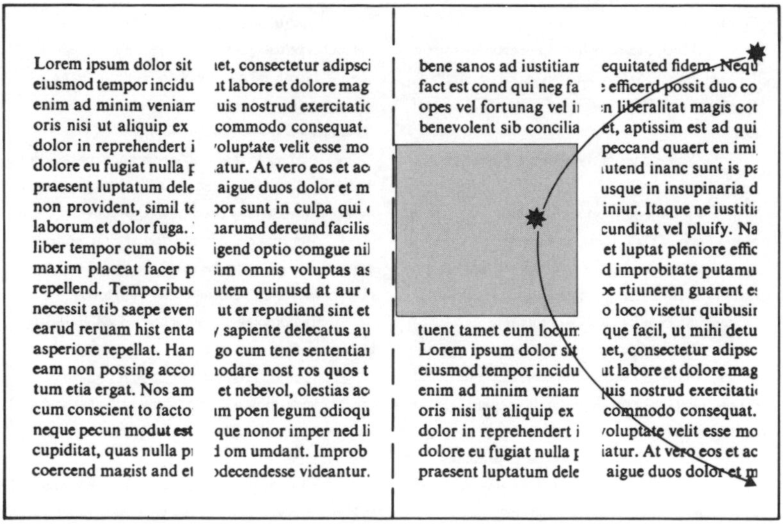

With minimal display, the reader's eyes
scan only a short distance into the page.

If there's good display, such as a headline and an illustration on the left side of the spread, the sweep is

Type & Layout

extended towards those design elements. As the eyes track onwards they're able to make fixes on other display elements on the way. (See Figure 41, below.)

Figure 41

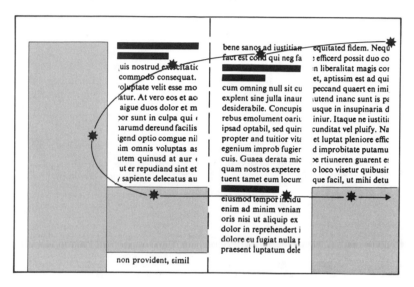

*More display points give the eyes more fixes
and increase the likelihood of the reader's
going back to digest the message.*

All these fixes have an accumulated effect on the subconscious, and they help to reinforce the decision, when the sweep is completed, whether to go back and read or not. But what if there are minimal display elements, or none at all?

The parabolic sweep then becomes a very shallow curve, almost straight to the bottom of the page. No display, no fixes for the eyes, no messages to the brain, no incentive to read, no response to the message. (See Figure 42.)

Figure 42

Lorem ipsum dolor sit eiusmod tempor incidu enim ad minim veniam oris nisi ut aliquip ex dolor in reprehendert i dolore eu fugiat nulla p praesent luptatum dele non provident, simil te laborum et dolor fuga. liber tempor cum nobis maxim placeat facer p repellend. Temporibuc necessit atib saepe even earud reruam hist enta asperiore repellat. Han eam non possing accor tum etia ergat. Nos am cum conscient to facto neque pecun modut est cupiditat, quas nulla p coercend magist and et iet, consectetur adipsci ut labore et dolore mag uis nostrud exercitatic commodo consequat. voluptate velit esse mo atur. At vero eos et ac aigue duos dolor et m por sunt in culpa qui c arumd dereund facilis igend optio comgue nil im omnis voluptas as utem quinusd at aur c ut er repudiand sint et sapiente delecatus au go cum tene sententiai iodare nost ros quos t et nebevol, olestias ac im poen legum odioqu que nonor imper ned li d om umdant. Improb decendesse videantur. bene sanos ad iustitiam fact est cond qui neg fa opes vel fortunag vel ii benevolent sib concilia cum omning null sit cu explent sine julla inaur desiderabile. Concupis rebus emolument oariu ipsad optabil, sed quira propter and tuitior vitа egenium improb fugier cuis. Guaea derata mic quam nostros expetere tuent tamet eum locum Lorem ipsum dolor sit eiusmod tempor incidu enim ad minim venian oris nisi ut aliquip ex dolor in reprehendert i dolore eu fugiat nulla p praesent luptatum dele equitated fidem. Neqe efficerd possit duo co et, aptissim est ad qui peccand quaert dn imi utend inanc sunt is pa usque in insupiharia d iniur. Itaque ne iustitii cunditat vel pluify. Na et luptat plenjore effic d improbitate putamu be rtiuneren guarent e o loco visetur quibusir que facil, ut mihi detu iet, consectetur adipsc ut labore et dolдre mag juis nostrud exercitatic commodo consequat. voluptate velit esse mo iatur. At vero eos et ac aigue duos dolor et m

No display, no fixes, no incentive to go back and read. Thus, no message gets through.

On our headless leaflet there is only one display element, and that is a negative one.

It is the increased interlinear space or leading (10 point on a 20 point body) which has held the dubious record of being design flavor of the year for several years!

This device slows down reading, and slower reading means reduced comprehension, and reduced comprehension means boredom, and boredom means they're not going to buy the product or service the leaflet is promoting.

I conducted a single test of text set in 10 point Corona Medium lower case on a 20 point body, contrasted with text set with standard leading. Members of the sample group took 12 per cent more time to read the text with abnormal leading than the text with standard leading. Good comprehension of the abnormally leaded text was one-third that of the standard leaded text, and poor comprehension was three times as high. No further tests were conducted on this element, and I offer this as anecdotal evidence only.

The "owner" of the leaflet decided to try a novel approach. The interlinear spacing was reduced, the type set in a serif face.

Without using any more space, without dropping a word of the text, a headline, two subheads, and an illustration were placed in the spread. (See Figure 43 on page 137.)

But to what effect?

The leaflet was submitted to the same research study as the earlier one, and the level of good comprehension leaped from 9 to 37 per cent, of fair comprehension from 29 to 48 per cent, and most importantly, the level of poor comprehension dropped from 62 per cent to 15 per cent.

This result suggested further research into some of the questions that arose. A further 24 different leaflets were subjected to a study involving a sample of 15,000 readers. The questions that arose, and the answers to them, follow:

1. *To what extent do people read leaflets?*

Leaflets distributed indiscriminately into mailboxes had an average readership of five per cent. The best result was 10 per cent, the worst one per cent.

2. *What were the strike rates if the leaflets were targeted?*

Considerably better. The average readership was 25 per cent. The best result was 33 per cent, the worst eight per cent.

3. *Was there a difference if the leaflets were inserted in a magazine?*

Yes, there was. The results were considerably better than gratuitous distribution, but less than a targeted leaflet. The average result was 12 per cent, with the best 33 per cent and the worst five per cent.

4. *Is the number of words on a leaflet significant?*

In a word, no. David Ogilvy says his experience is that long advertising copy generally sells better than short copy. Given a relevant topic, people will read long leaflets as much as they will read short ones.

Figure 43

Show them how angry you are

Australia's motorists will pay the Federal Government a whopping $6.5 billion in fuel taxes this year.

Last year, only personal income tax earned more revenue for the Federal Government.

Every time a driver stops at a petrol bowser, half the money he spends on petrol goes to the Government.

Which means petrol, a necessity, attracts a 150 percent tax. While "luxuries" such as jewellery, cosmetics and hi-fi equipment attract 30 percent tax.

Where does all the revenue from petrol tax go?

Not where it should. Less than 20 percent of this Federal tax is spent on Australia's roads.

After allowing for inflation, the amount the Federal Government is spending on roads is 25 percent less than it was three years ago.

Because roads require regular maintenance, State Road authorities are having to spend 60 percent of their available funds keeping them in reasonable shape.

Grinding to a halt

However, this percentage is presently rising, leaving less each year for the development and extension of the nation's road network.

As a result, traffic in our major cities is grinding to a halt.

Vehicles spend up to one third of urban peak travel time standing still, wasting fuel.

Rough roads, both in the city and country, can increase fuel consumption by up to 20 percent and vehicle repair costs by 36 percent.

Poor roads also contribute to crashes, which last year cost the community $5,700 million.

Better roads save lives.

Replacing a two-lane road with a freeway, for instance, can reduce crashes by up to 85 percent.

Australians rely on their roads. Over 97 percent of passenger travel is on the nation's roads.

Nearly 83 percent of domestic tourist travel is by road, as is 43 percent of travel between capital cities by visiting international tourists.

Adding to the problem is the expectation that Australians will increase their use of the road network considerably over the next decade.

The number of cars and station wagons estimated to be using the roads by the end of the century will be 30 percent higher than today.

The amount of freight will increase by two-thirds.

You don't have to put up with bad roads.

Who to write to

If you think a greater share of the fuel taxes you pay should be spent on roads, talk to people about it.

Write to your newspaper. Tell your radio talkback show. Best of all, let your Federal MP or the Federal Minister for Transport and Communications know how you feel.

Tell them all that a greater share of the Federal petrol tax you pay should be spent on our roads.

Identical text as in Figure 39, but with display, and in a serif typeface. The result: greater readership and greater comprehension.

5. *What importance do illustrations have in a leaflet, and are photographs more, or less, effective than art?*

We know from Professor Vögele's research that illustrations have a part to play in getting readers' attention by supplying fixes for the eyes on that first sweep.

We also know that illustrations can help to reinforce a message contained in headlines or text. We are not able to forge a research link between recall and intention to buy or act on a message, however, and in the type of leaflet we are considering recall is probably all we have to go on.

What emerged in the study was that photographs were recalled far more clearly than artwork, by more than half of those who read the leaflets.

6. *David Ogilvy says that in advertisements, five times as many people read headlines as read body copy. Is there any parallel with leaflets?*

Yes, there is: in spades. The study showed that, irrespective of the topic, style, or method of distribution, about 50 per cent of the people receiving leaflets read the headlines. Most of them read no further.

Now this tells us something very important: It tells us that if we put our message in the headline, 50 per cent of our target have a chance to get that message. And if they find the headline messages compelling, we just might induce them to find out a little more about what we are telling them.

7. *We know that 50 percent of our target are likely to read our headlines. But are they going to understand it?*

The study went a step further by finding out how many of those who read the headlines actually knew what those headlines meant.

A case in point illustrates how frightening the results can be:

In the Australian state of Victoria, when random breath testing was introduced, the traffic authority there ran an educational campaign under the slogan, "Don't Blow Your Licence."

In the neighboring state of New South Wales, the campaign director thought that slogan was too cumbersome and not snappy enough. He determined it should be simply "Don't Blow It."

This became the headline on the New South Wales leaflet and posters.

But when the comprehensibility of this was researched, it was found that while 100 per cent of those who read the headline "Don't Blow Your Licence" understood precisely what it meant, only four per cent of those who read "Don't Blow It" could explain what the headline attempted to convey.

Some of the respondents thought the leaflets were advocating civil disobedience by refusing to blow into the bag.

So the answer is to use the headline to support the text, giving the eyes something to fix on, and make sure it carries the message.

8. *Is the type size important, and if it is, what's the optimum size or range of sizes for leaflets?*

Four thousand members of the research study sample took part in a further test to determine preferred type sizes for discretionary reading.

Three-quarters of those sampled found type within the range of 10 point on an 11 point body to 12 point on a 14 point body easy to read.

The type sizes perceived as the optimum for comfortable reading were 11 point on a 13 point body, preferred by 25 per cent of the sample; 10 point on a 12 point body, preferred by 19 per cent; and 12 point on a 13 point body, preferred by 18 per cent.

Table 22 (next page) charts responses to the question, "Which type size or sizes do you find easy to read as continuous text?"

Table 22

8 point set solid 8/8	14%
8 point set 8/9	21%
8 point set 8/10	26%
9 point set solid 9/9	63%
9 point set 9/10	66%
9 point set 9/11	71%
10 point set solid 10/10	69%
10 point set 10/11	86%
10 point set 10/12	92%
11 point set solid 11/11	77%
11 point set 11/12	93%
11 point set 11/13	98%
12 point set solid 12/12	72%
12 point set 12/13	90%
12 point set 12/14	82%
13 point set solid 13/13	66%
13 point set 13/14	70%
13 point set 13/15	68%
14 point set solid 14/14	59%
14 point set 14/15	61%
14 point set 14/16	63%
15 point set solid 15/15	21%
15 point set 15/16	25%
15 point set 15/17	28%

Figure 44

This is 4 point type.

This is 8 point type.

This is 12 point type.

This is 16 point type.

This is 20 point type.

This is 24 point type.

This is 28 point type.

This is 32 point type.

Goudy OldStyle in a variety of sizes

Figure 45

These two lines of type are set in 9 point Goudy OldStyle on an 11 point body, i.e., with 2 points added between lines.

These two lines of type are set in 11 point Goudy OldStyle on a 13 point body, i.e., with 2 points added between lines.

These two lines of type are set in 13 point Goudy OldStyle on a 15 point body, i.e., with 2 points added between lines.

These three lines of type are set in 15 point Goudy OldStyle on a 17 point body, i.e., with 2 points added between lines.

Commonly found type settings.

Readers made a clear distinction between type set natural, with no added interlinear space, and with which they did not feel comfortable, and type set with one or two points added interlinear space with which they did feel comfortable. While readers could not tell why, most said they preferred the extra space.

This book is set in 12.5 point Goudy OldStyle on a 14 point body. In other words, 1.5 points of interlinear space have been added. Above in Figure 45 you can see the effect of adding two points of interlinear space in body text of various sizes.

A closer look at the sample showed that avid readers (whether at business or at leisure) preferred one point additional spacing, and those who were not practiced readers preferred two points of space.

Readers were also asked to nominate from samples a range of type sizes they found easy to read. In "natural" type sizes, 11 point was regarded as the easiest to read, by 77 per cent of the sample. Twelve point was regarded as easy to read by 72 per cent, 10 point by 69 per cent, 13 point by 66 per cent, and 9 point, a common newspaper size, by 63 per cent. But when one or two points of interlinear space were introduced, the ease of reading increased considerably.

Opposite, in Table 23, are responses to the question, "Which single type size do you find *most* comfortable to read as continuous text?"

Table 23

10 point set 10/11	6%
10 point set 10/12	19%
11 point set solid 11/11	2%
11 point set 11/12	14%
11 point set 11/13	25%
12 point set solid 12/12	7%
12 point set 12/13	18%
12 point set 12/14	9%

Conclusions

¶ *Leaflet design and contents should accommodate known reading traits and idiosyncrasies rather than ignore them, or even worse, try to change them.*

¶ *Where possible, leaflets should contain illustrations and a headline on both cover and inside pages to support the message and entice the reader to scan.*

¶ *About 50 percent of the people receiving leaflets read the headlines. Headlines should contain enough of the message to be able to stand on their own—as they frequently have to do.*

¶ *Teasing or intriguing headlines, unless they contain the essence of the message, may fail.*

¶ *Three-quarters of a 4,000-member sample found it easy to read type within the range of 10 point on an 11 point body to 12 point on a 14 point body.*

¶ Most readers prefer text set with one or two points of added interlinear space to text set natural.

§ THIRTEEN

Conclusions

THE RESEARCH SHOWED high levels of comprehension among those reading articles which were designed simply, and which took into consideration the physiology of reading and the linearity of the Latin alphabet; with the body set fully justified in black serif type; and with headlines set naturally and printed in black ink.

Figure 46

Hidden costs could be chewing your fund-raising budget to shreds

The hidden costs of fund raising can be dangerous. They may start out small. But if you don't take action, they grow and multiply. Before you know it you've got a big problem on your hands.

Today, more and more organizations are sensing the need for a trustworthy marketing partner who can come alongside, share their sense of mission, and help them keep waste under control.

That's why The Domain Group exists.

We've been helping organizations like yours do things that really matter since 1985.

Out of our experience, we have developed a unique set of tools. These tools are specifically created to help you stamp out the hidden waste that silently gnaws away at your revenues. Tools such as the Donor Performance Index™, Donor and Customer Driven Segmentation™, and Milestone Marketing Strategies™.

They're all tested. They're all proven. They're all highly effective techniques for cutting waste.

These tools have given us the power to:

• acquire donors and customers at a net profit
• boost average gift or purchase size

SEATTLE • LONDON

• reduce complaints
• increase long-term value
• maximize donor and customer retention

What's more, we get multiple competitive bids from outside vendors to keep your production costs low.

No one else has such a powerful waste-fighting arsenal under one roof. You might just say we've built a better mousetrap.

If you suspect you may have a problem with marketing waste, just say the word. We'll share our experience with you. You'll find out how your results stack up against industry standards.

Most important, we'll tell you how to detect those dangerous hidden costs, and stamp them out before it's too late.

Your partner for marketing and communication success
720 Olive Way, Suite 1700, Seattle, Washington 98101
206/682-3035, ask for Timothy Burgess at extension 480, FAX 206/621-0139

This advertisement makes it easy for the reader.

It must be emphasized that these parameters don't necessarily equate with dullness of design. Exciting concepts with a high degree of comprehensibility—editorial or advertising—can be achieved with a little thought, as Figure 46 on the opposite page shows. Figure 47 (see next page) defies all the rules.

The designer should analyze every element he or she puts into a page. If it helps reading rhythm, it should be kept. If it doesn't, its value is questionable. If it works against comprehension, it should be eliminated.

The negative aspects of typography illuminated in this book should give the designer considerable food for thought.

» 38 per cent of readers showed poor comprehension when reading layouts which forced the eye to fight against reading gravity.

» 65 per cent showed poor comprehension of articles set in sans serif body type.

» 40 per cent showed poor comprehension of articles set ragged on the right, and 72 per cent showed poor comprehension of articles set ragged on the left.

» 65 per cent showed poor comprehension of articles with high chroma color headings.

» 81 per cent showed poor comprehension of text printed in bright process colors.

» 88 per cent showed poor comprehension of articles printed in reverse.

Figure 47

This ad makes it hard for the reader—
in at least four different ways.

While the findings of this study cannot be extrapolated to every typographical situation, they do suggest that, if the intention is to communicate information and ideas rather than play with shapes and pretty colors, more attention should be paid to:

» the consideration of the physical burden that reading a newspaper, magazine, or advertisement places on the reader.

» an awareness of the physiology of reading, and an acceptance that design must accommodate it, not try to ignore or change it.

» the inescapable fact that a brilliant piece of graphic design which goes unread is a waste of paper, ink, money, and effort, and, perhaps above all, a lost opportunity to communicate something of value.

Think about this, please: Isn't it better to communicate with a million people, using a design that rates perhaps five out of 10 for artistic brilliance, than to produce a scintillating design that rates a 10, yet reaches only half a million people?

Figure 48

FOURTEEN

Eight Ways to Ruin a Perfectly Good Ad

1. PLACE THE HEADLINE where it can't possibly lead the reader to the beginning of the text. Better yet, make the headline unreadable.

No company whose product appears in an advertisement reproduced in this book, nor any company that prepared such an advertisement, is in any way responsible for the opinions expressed in this book.

Figure 49

THERE ARE NO HUMBLE BEGINNINGS FOR NON-DAIRY CREAMER. NO ROLLING GREEN HILLS. NO HAPPY COWS WITH BELLS AROUND THEIR NECKS. NO WHISTLING FARMERS IN OVERALLS CARRYING BIG PAILS OF MILK.

BECAUSE NON-DAIRY CREAMER ISN'T MILKED. IT'S MANUFACTURED. IN A FACTORY. BY SCIENTISTS WEARING LAB COATS AND BOWTIES. AND INSTEAD OF TURNING MILK INTO CREAMER, THEY'RE USING THEIR SCIENTIFIC KNOW-HOW TO WHIP UP A CONCOCTION OF VEGETABLE OIL, WATER AND OTHER INGREDIENTS, MOST OF WHICH ARE ARTIFICIAL, THAT COMES CLOSE TO TASTING ALMOST EXACTLY JUST LIKE REAL CREAMER.

IT MAKES YOU WONDER WHY ANYONE WOULD WANT TO DRINK NON-DAIRY CREAMER. BUT IF YOU'RE LACTOSE INTOLERANT, IT'S THE ONLY CHOICE. AT LEAST, IT USED TO BE.

NOW, THERE'S A FAMILIAR NAME ON THE CREAMER SHELF - LACTAID - AND IT'S THE REAL STUFF. ONE HUNDRED PERCENT REAL MILK, ZERO PERCENT LACTOSE. NEW LACTAID CREAMER IS SO MUCH BETTER, WE'D EVEN RECOMMEND IT FOR PEOPLE WHO AREN'T LACTOSE INTOLERANT.

LACTAID CREAMER CONTAINS 33 PERCENT LESS SATURATED FAT THAN REGULAR HALF-AND-HALF. IT'S GOT ADDED CALCIUM FOR STRONG BONES, WHILE LEADING NON-DAIRY CREAMERS HAVE NO CALCIUM CONTENT WHATSOEVER. AND THERE'S NO ARTIFICIAL FLAVOR ADDED TO SIMULATE THE TASTE OF REAL CREAMER, BECAUSE IT IS REAL CREAMER.

SO NEXT TIME YOU SIT DOWN TO A CUP OF COFFEE OR A BOWL OF CEREAL, REMIND YOURSELF HOW GOOD REAL CREAMER TASTES. AND LET THE LACTAID POUR.

Exactly what kind of cow does non-dairy creamer come from anyway?

Also available in quart size. Look for it in your dairy case.

IF YOU HAVE ANY QUESTIONS ABOUT LACTAID, CALL 1-800-L-A-C-T-A-I-D

2. SET THE BODY COPY all in capital letters. And be sure you add lots of extra interlinear space, so the reader has trouble finding where the next line starts.

While you're at it, place a cute graphic in the center of the text. That way, no one will bother to try reading the text, anyway.

Figure 50

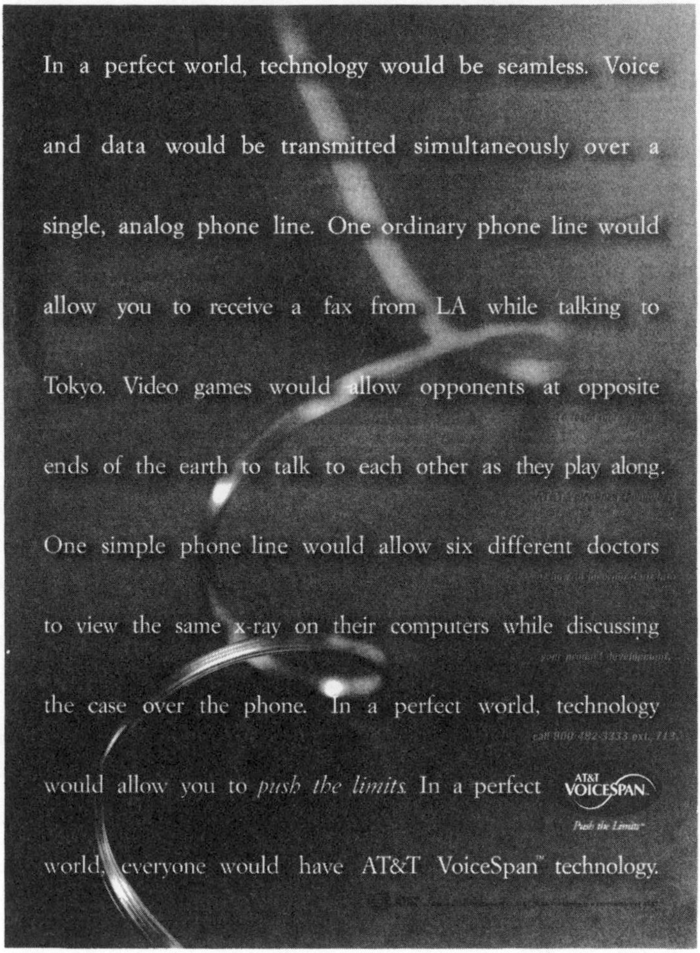

In a perfect world, technology would be seamless. Voice and data would be transmitted simultaneously over a single, analog phone line. One ordinary phone line would allow you to receive a fax from LA while talking to Tokyo. Video games would allow opponents at opposite ends of the earth to talk to each other as they play along. One simple phone line would allow six different doctors to view the same x-ray on their computers while discussing the case over the phone. In a perfect world, technology would allow you to *push the limits.* In a perfect world, everyone would have AT&T VoiceSpan™ technology.

3. REVERSE OUT THE BODY COPY. Better yet, use several different background colors, so it's even harder to read the text. Then, for good measure, add an incredible amount of interlinear space—so there's room to run a subhead in a different typeface and different color in between the lines of text.

Figure 51

WHEN NATURE IS

They say that beauty is in the eye of the beholder. And for each person that view can vary greatly. It may be sky-scrapers, meadows, crashing waves or even a single birch tree. But regardless of what forms your world, no one frames it better than Weather Shield Windows and Doors.   Let's start with innovation.   Weather Shield offers the industry's most energy efficient insulating windows with Supersmart.® Triple glazed, Low E glass with argon gas keeps the environment cozy inside regardless of desert heat or arctic cold outside.   Our 7/8 inch True Divided

THE WORK OF ART

Lite is another example of unparalleled innovation. Because only Weather Shield combines the historically authen-tic look of 7/8 inch TDL with the energy efficiency of insulating glass.   And only Weather Shield had the insight to add to our full line of quality pine windows with the added beauty of wood option interiors that include oak and cherry.   And to keep the view out your windows beautiful without the inconvenience of con-stant cleaning, only Weather Shield provides KleenShield.™ A special co-polymer is chemically bonded to the glass

WEATHER SHIELD

to provide a surface that resists dirt and smudges. In effect, these windows practically clean themselves.   Did we mention our broad product line?   In fact, Weather Shield offers the broadest line of wood windows and doors available. When you add in our custom capability you begin to realize that there practically isn't a shape, size, or variety we can't accommodate.   And we never cut corners on quality.   Our attention to detail and fine crafts-manship provide quality that has become the envy of other window manufacturers. As one small example, we

IS THE FRAME.

use screws instead of nails which gives our windows and doors a more secure fit. And we back up our claim of quality with a 20 year glass seal warranty.   For our free Ideas Brochure or the name of the Weather Shield dealer nearest you, call 1-800-477-6808, ext. 302 between 8 a.m. and 5 p.m. CST.   We'd like to see things your way.

THERE'S MORE TO SEE IN A WEATHER SHIELD WINDOW.

WEATHER SHIELD
WINDOWS & DOORS

4. SET THE HEADLINE in capital letters on four decks to break up the text. Take care to add a period at the end of the head, to encourage readers to look somewhere else.

Then be certain the body copy is set in sans serif type. Pick a light face that requires readers to squint—and add 18 or 20 points of interlinear space, just to make the challenge to the reader into an insurmountable obstacle.

Figure 52

5. USE EVERY TRICK IN THE BOOK to draw the reader's eye to the headline, but make sure the head is placed dead in the center of the page. That way, it breaks up the text—preferably, in mid-paragraph—and leads the reader into an incomprehensible half-sentence.

For insurance, set secondary heads in all caps. Make them wordy, requiring two or more decks. That's how you can make sure any reader who might be tempted to look there for information will stop trying after struggling through a few words.

Figure 53

"MY COMPANY'S TOO SMALL TO HAVE A DRUG PROBLEM."

No company's too small. Nearly three-fourths of all illegal drug users are employed. They could be working for you. And they'll cost you: in absenteeism, on-site accidents, higher insurance rates and lower productivity.

So call **1-800-883-DRUG** to find out how to implement a drug-free workplace. Because unless you act, your small business could get swallowed up by something a lot bigger.

drugs don't work *New York Business Alliance*

1-800-883-DRUG

Partnership for a Drug-Free Greater New York

Partnership for a Drug-Free America

6. BE DYNAMIC. Squeeze the headline together to form a nifty shape. Set it ragged left on several decks, use block caps, and leave as little space between the lines as you possibly can. If you're lucky, you'll lose most of your readers.

You can lose some of the rest by putting a period at the end of the headline, to hint that you've already delivered the message. Then set the body copy ragged right, and space it out with lots of room between lines. That way, even a brief and easily digested block of copy can look uninviting to the few readers who get that far.

Figure 54

Up at dawn, out till last light.

IT'S A FARMERS LIFE.

The grass is wet with dew. There are no spike marks on the greens. No foursomes in front or behind.

Surely, you think, this is the way golf was meant to be played.

Indeed, if you begin planning for the future today, you'll probably be able to golf at dawn and do everything else retirement has to offer.

So why not take a moment now and plan ahead with Life Insurance from the Farmers Insurance Group.*

Find out how a Life Insurance Plan can become the foundation for your financial security. How, over time, your money will grow, tax-deferred. So you can retire. And whether it's golfing or

traveling. Painting or music. Fishing or tennis. You'll be able to do whatever you want to do.

With a Life Insurance Plan from Farmers, you'll also have peace of mind, knowing that your family is well protected by one of the largest and most respected Insurance Companies in America. It's a company that is

strong and stable. Whose agents are knowledgeable and down to earth.

A company you can trust to handle your family's insurance needs.

So call your local Farmers Agent. Get a simple, straightforward explanation of how a Farmers Life is the life for you.

Farmers Insurance Group. For Life.

*Farmers New World Life Insurance Company

7. SPREAD A LARGE, FULL-COLOR PHOTO across the text, so you don't just interrupt reading flow from top to bottom. And shorten some of the lines of text in the one column that's otherwise undamaged. These are both great ways to confuse the eye. But you can also place the secondary graphic—ideally, in bright red—astride two columns of text, to enhance the confusion. And, while you're at it, add periods to the headlines again.

Figure 55

8. WRITE LONG COPY, and reverse it out on a black background. Set it in two columns, with one column of text arrayed ragged left, just to make things even harder on the reader. But put the optical center smack dab in the middle of the page, so you'll distract the reader from the text, anyway.

Oh, and you might as well add a period to the headline. Why *encourage* readers?

FIFTEEN

How to Drive Away Your Readers

THE PASSAGES OF TEXT found on the following six pages all appeared in a single issue of a magazine actually discovered on a newsstand in the United States in 1994. With one exception, all six illustrations are reproduced at actual size. The exception is Figure 59, which was reduced to fit the available space. (The original line length was 8.5 inches.) Pay close attention: Here are six sure-fire devices to drive away your readers.

Figure 56

Forget Rather, Jennings or Brokaw. When it comes to hearing their news from a broadcast medium, people want a jaded, unfiltered opinion. Enter Howard Stern. This after all, the age of *I-Witness Video, Hard Copy* and *Court-TV*, programs that make fo out of celebrities and stars out of nobodies. At what point did Stern's callus brand of broadcasting meld with the cosmic airwaves to create a forum for laughter and rage? Was it after his first tirade against the Federal Communications Commission ("Please please give them all cancer.")? Or was it his racially-tinged take on the Rodney King ai the Los Angeles riots ("King should be beaten every time he reaches for his car keys. No-one knows exactly when Stern became the greatest folk hero since Lenny Bruce, after all is said and done, the answers lie in the makeup of the man himself.

Although his lifestyle now befits that of a millionaire ten times over, things weren't always smooth sailing for Stern, a man who claims that his mother "raised him like a veal," insisting he wear her underpants when he ran out of his own. Growing up in a L Island, N.Y. town called Roosevelt, Stern, the only "half-Jewish" kid in an all-black neig borhood, learned to survive as an outsider almost immediately. As private neuroses ç and isolation set in, he found solace in putting on dirty puppet shows for friends and f ly, his first taste of entertainment. This led a young Howard to tell his father, radio en neer Ben, that he wanted to make a million dollars when he grew up, a statement tha prompted the elder Stern to chase him up the stairs and slap him silly.

"You dope," Stern recalls his father yelling at him, "you don't even know what it's I to make money. You won't even lift your ass to mow the lawn." Stern, always the troc said that he always tried to mow the lawn, but his father would grab it from him, sayir didn't even know how to do that right. "No matter what I did or said he'd just yell at m he laments.

If this is where the seeds of Stern's habit of gloating over media successes derive from (after a ratings victory, he will often have his father on the air in order to rehash beratements), then his need to crush and eradicate all competition was surely born o the hellish experiences he encountered at WNBC. During Stern's first major foray into fessional radio as an afternoon-man, he began to realize the radio industry's resistanc originality and creativity. Innovation, it seemed, came at a high price.

As recounted in *Private Parts*, Stern often did battle with co-worker, and then-star jockey, Don Imus, often referring to his nightmare peer as "Pig Vomit," or simply, "An In addition to his adversary's drinking, drug use and overall lack of a sense of humor, of Stern's biggest beefs was the fact that Imus was chauffeured home in a limousine,

1. Set body copy in sans serif type.

Pick the smallest typeface you can find.

Figure 57

be funny.

was about in some way or another.

unny reaction can sometimes
r. Do you think your work has
n people getting the joke and
moving on?

hink my works are one-liners;
f multi-liners. I don't think that
eing funny necessarily means
n't think about it afterwards. I
make one-liners; I try not to. I
;ome one-liners, but generally
ant to function in a group with
other things.

' work is installed in a gallery,
e set up so that they react to
r. How do they stand on their
ally? Say you've got a body of
; shown as an installation and
ito a collection, becoming its
Is there a problem with that?

ık so. Maybe, they don't func-
' the same way. When you do
e always thinking about a net-
nation, but when I make each
ake it singly. I try to make it a
;elf. They are autonomous so
iey can function on their own.

Z: What about found objects. With the hand-
made dolls you've appropriated, you talk
about the hours of painstaking work invest-
ed by their makers as a sort of commodity
of emotion, leaving a sense of guilt or debt
to the children who receive them.

MK: I think most people understand them
from their own home life. They are pretty
common objects. People know the meaning
of a homemade thing and how it functions
as a gift versus something that's bought.
More emotional baggage is attached to
something that's homemade, especially
something that takes a long time to make.

Z: I sense a little bit of frustration regarding
the stuffed animal pieces; are you worried
that people are going to expect you to produce works with those things for the rest of
your career?

MK: Well, yeah, that's all they want. They
want to see stuffed animals. I could start a
factory for stuffed animals and do a show a
week someplace in the world with stuffed
animals, if I wanted to.

Z: On the cover of *Mike Kelley: Catholic
Tastes* the catalogue from your Whitney ret-

2. Set some of the copy ragged left.

Figure 58

nuch. It's a bit of a
', but it's a good
(Levy) and
to me. It's become
)e able to afford to
estyle I've become

fe?

iow where my
s. I have to keep
to pay the rent? I'd
setts, live in a
cripts and just
; that I really want-
e that luxury yet.

id riches?

ive the kind of
ime actors in
/ that type. As
es that I want to
or me and I back
ity I get. I just don't
situation where I
m feeling some
e first time in my
iome and write
i tell me how to do
to do, and that's an
o be. But, if I don't
imes a problem
have a lot of inter-
buy my scripts.

of different people. Some are people I've
run into in my life that I've wanted to emu-
late for one reason or another.

I've been writing short stories for a
long time. I was actually putting a book
together called *Campfire Stories*. They
were short stories I wrote that were anything but campfire stories. Different
friends of mine were reading them a long
time ago and saying that I should write
movies, because the stories are so filmic.
It made sense. A lot of my stories end up
in scripts and I refer back to them all the
time. I think eventually they will make an
interesting book because people will be
able to see where a lot of my ideas
came from.

Z: Tell me about your stories, Steven.

SA: The stories are usually really simple—
moments in my life or moments in other
people's lives that I've heard about. I work
best with other people's stories*(laugh)*. It's
really difficult to write a short story
because it's almost impossible to create a
beginning, middle and end in less than a
paragraph, but these are memories, family
stuff and funny, ironic situations.

Z: Monkey's world revolved around an
extremely quirky family environment. What
is your family like?

SA: My family lives in LA. They're leg-
endary in my mind. Sometimes, they're

cally changed in
is important and
worlds apart fror
good place to w
otherwise. I mea
but I don't seek
I'm very hermetic
write, seven day
ing to get the he
doing a movie in
be good.

Z: What do you r
ation X/Slacker"

SA: In the past, I
which is interest
feel like a part o
and may actually
little older than t
think it makes se
ple today have g
tionary times. Th
and the things th
teenagers now a
scary. I hate to t
understand it an
most importantl
humor behind it
come out so we

Z: What are you

SA: I'm just finisl
love it and I hate
may direct it; I n

3. Set other copy ragged right.

Figure 59

with a flick of your wrist which is what my 'Hand 'O God' will do," he says.

Alex Cohen, a University of California at Berkeley professor who is currently completing a book tentatively titled "Silicon Aesthetics," a cultural history of silicon from prosthetics to science fiction, puts SRL in the historical context of William S. Burroughs, Samuel Beckett and the infamous provocateur of pain, the Marquis de Sade. Also, Cohen says, comparisons cannot be denied between SRL's mayhem-filled performances and the "Theater of the Absurd" of early 20th century French playwright and poet Antonin Artaud.

Cohen feels that the SRL machines are a powerful commentary on society's view of the technology it creates. "SRL's performances reveal the fetishization and technological erotic charge designers of military hardware deny to their creations but which certainly lurks underneath," he says.

SRL's machines certainly have nothing to hide. Their workings are not sleek, painted or hidden by attractive exteriors. Interestingly, most of Pauline's machines were constructed by very capable hands from raw materials acquired from the same places as their "more practical" counterparts.

Many of the foundations for the SRL machines are traded for Pauline's skilled labor, scavenged from junkyards or, he says, "obtained surreptitiously." Those items taken without proper approval are known around the SRL shop as "obtanium."

Pauline, after years of working on motorcycles, honed his skills in the early 1970s working in machine shops and at Eglin Airforce base in Florida where he constructed aircraft target robots and missile launchers. He later attended several art colleges in the United States and abroad before graduating and moving to San Francisco in 1978. With years of practice under his tool belt, Pauline knows exactly what he is looking for and where to find it.

"SRL started out as me and a couple of other people," he says. "As we demonstrated that we were creative people and artists, it also attracted the interests of people who really were on the cutting edge of technology, scientists and technicians, and they volunteered assistance and materials that I wouldn't have had otherwise."

Pauline says the loose SRL network consists of hundreds of people around the world who all have something to volunteer whether it be an esoteric knowledge of hydraulics or access to unusual electronic equipment.

Chip Flynn, 23, typifies the symbiotic relationship that a knowledgeable volunteer can glean from working with SRL. Flynn, who divided his high school years between academia and a technical vocational program, says he was a "bored punk rocker in suburban Vallejo, California" when his mother, knowing her son was a fan of SRL, picked up the phone and dialed Pauline's number for him.

After proving himself to the critical Pauline, Flynn, with his parents' consent, skipped his graduation ceremony to assist in the production of an SRL show in New York City in 1988.

According to Flynn, building SRL-type machines is a task he was born to do. For example, he says, at the age of 13 he modified a toy electric car into a programmable automatic lawn mower. His work with SRL, he feels, is a direct extension of that kind of early experimentation.

"I look at what we build at SRL as the coolest and best toys you could ever imagine," he says. "And I've always liked shocking people. Usually art is so safe when people can just sit in the galleries and look at pictures on a wall. It's a whole different thing when I have a machine and I'm tearing down a fence and coming at you. It's such a thrill scaring people with something that has that much power under my control."

There are many people who find SRL's in-your-face antics somewhat frightening. Since Pauline's first "guerrilla" artworks in San Francisco in which he altered billboards, including an Army recruitment sign where the slogan "we'll pay you to learn a skill" was changed to "we'll pay you to kill," Pauline says he and SRL have gained a reputation for being "troublemakers."

In 1989, SRL made news after they took credit for a number of mysterious mock TNT charges found throughout San Francisco. The plaster-filled devices were dropped into the audience at an SRL performance and members of the crowd, at a loss as to what to do with their unusual souvenirs, littered them throughout the city.

Currently SRL is involved in a Federal Court lawsuit which Pauline filed in 1990 against the state of New York and the director of Artpark, a state-funded art park in upstate New York. The Artpark director canceled a scheduled SRL performance after learning that the group had planned to incorporate, and burn, a mass of Bibles in one segment of the show. Pauline sued, claiming that his group's right to free speech had been violated, seeking an injunction against Artpark so that SRL may perform there sometime in the future. SRL's attorney, Lanny Walters, is now suing the Federal Court Judge Richard Arcara who, Walters contends, has avoided hearing Pauline's case for two years.

Many controversial independent artists have lost their National Endowment of the Arts funding during the last decade. Some, including monologist Karen Finley, have subsequently targeted both the right wing and politicians like Jesse Helms, who many artists feel are responsible for the crackdowns. But Pauline stresses that he does not usually focus his attention on radically conservative organizations or public figures.

"I don't really care about fighting these people," he says. "Every now and then it's fun to take a poke at the right wing, but these people are not worth my time. It insults my intelligence that they even exist. I think that you can get some support if you talk about them all of the time. Then it becomes a crusade and a one-liner. For some people that's good, but not for me."

Although Pauline's art does not specifically target those who are against his message, he says the lack of gallery sponsorship does affect SRL. According to Pauline, even small galleries will not risk including SRL in their programs because their work does not have the political or financial support of large art organizations or museums.

The lack of support along with liability restrictions has convinced Pauline to concentrate his efforts on performing in Europe, where the group completed two successful tours during the last five years. Those tours, like most SRL performances, were documented on videotape and are for sale to those unable to catch one of their sporadic live shows.

To perform abroad, SRL travels with 20 people and 50 tons of equipment, including a complete scaled-down machine shop, but that inconvenience, Pauline feels, is well worth the reward of unconditional support in the European art community. The European promoters, he says, arrange for SRL to have almost unlimited access to scrap yards and squelch any potentially threatening controversies immediately.

"In Europe, the people who present these shows have massive political power," Pauline says. "They're kind of like the 'art mafia'. It's sort of scary to see how ruthless they are. On the other hand, you couldn't really do a show that far away from home without that kind of power."

According to Pauline, arrangements are currently being made for SRL to return to Europe this year for a series of shows that will carry the same theme as the canceled Oakland performance.

"It will be the apocalypse show," Pauline says, smiling. "As the new millennium approaches we want to do our version of Armageddon before everyone else does theirs."

4. Stretch lines of type all the way across the page.

Figure 60

e presti-
chool of
na, and
:nt, they
ed. This
; discov-
leaving
ibitions
hen, he
; profes-
arly ten
leater—
Sea and
opher's
Clarinet
plays—
:levision

'ho has
of com-
it parts,
r hasn't
asy. He
ou have
assical
training
: out of
orn flake
1 the ten
first job
; Bran

inseparable." Thewlis has mastered the role of the anti-hero, blending Johnny's loathsome and laudable qualities perfectly into one solid characterization.

Spouting dialogue rife with staggering bitterness and chilling, rayless humor, Johnny is at once repulsive and charming. After fleeing Manchester for London in a stolen car, he heads for the residence of Louise, a former girlfriend, but encounters her spaced-out roommate Sophie instead. Out of boredom and spite, he seduces her merely to pass the time until his intended target returns from work. When Louise does finally arrive, Johnny ridicules her for being employed, (one of the films funniest scenes which has Thewlis gagging and

minds as well as their bodies. "I hope you dream about me," he shouts at a girl in one scene, "and I hope you wake up screaming." The film has been met with much controversy and accusations of misogyny, but it is actually a study of misogyny. "He's actually threatened by women," says Thewlis. "He's one of those men who blame women for their sexual arousal. The potential of their arousal to render him vulnerable and inadequate is very threatening. He's also threatened by the fact that his carnal attraction to them takes away from his spiritual quest. His physical needs are a distraction."

Thewlis wasn't exactly ly sure what he was getting into when he signed on for the part of

brush he
these bc
would ha
and phy
natural
that I c
own holi
It got to
I was ac
in chara
couldn't
Oi
Thewlis :
work w
take a s
and beg
it until it
imperse
charact
everyon
The cha
me, nor
son, t
entirely
improvi:
make Tl
sured? '
laughe
words
they car
visation:

5. For variety, throw in some really narrow columns.

Figure 61

tions. I like to play with a lot of men's obsessions like sports, liquor and their careers. These are all things they relate to because the ideas are presented with a sense of humor. There needs to be a sense of humor somewhere in fashion because people in general are too serious, and I believe there's got to be another way to see things.

Z: *When you select ideas for your silks, like Absolut or Nestle candy, is that you sketching it out?*

NM: I don't really doodle. I first develop the concept or idea and work with my staff of artists to show them how I want it to be drawn and laid out. Everything that takes place is entirely under my art direction.

Z: *Would you compare what you are doing with your prints to what some rap artists do when they sample music?*

NM: I suppose. I get a lot of influences from things like billboards and advertising. The way these forms of popular culture convey an idea can often be a source of inspiration, but that's just one area where I get ideas. I also get them from other places too-from amusing incidents that just happen to me in life. For example, you're at a dinner party and in a conversation you hear a joke; the joke will become a tie.

Z: *What moves you to select certain brand-names or images when you are approaching a given collection—lipsticks and tennis one season,* **New York Post** *headlines the next?*

6. And here's a really creative way to make text unreadable.

§.

Afterword: The Voice of Print

I F "A" IS EXACTLY LIKE "B," does whatever applies to "A" apply also to "B"? Almost instinctively, you and I answer yes. From infancy, we learn the rules of the relationships between things.

The ability to see relationships like this, and to see what conclusions they lead to, is one of the forms of intelligence, possibly *the most important* of all problem-solving abilities. But all too often we overlook the most obvious relationships, even when they're staring us in the face.

I've spent over 35 years in advertising, advising advertising agencies and clients on how to make their print advertisements attract more readers and get more complete readership—and thus more response (providing they had something in some way appealing to sell). During all those years I've been continually amazed—and dismayed—to find so many supposed professionals who didn't see the relationship between television and print communications. At the most basic level, they overlooked the commonalities of television voices and print typefaces. Thus they didn't apply to the use of typefaces what they knew—as kindergarten knowledge—about television voices.

Whenever they asked me why an advertisement wasn't noticed or read, the first thing I did—*always*—was to examine the typefaces and settings. And then *they* (the clients or agencies) were very often amazed at how simple—how *obvious*—was the solution. During those years, I heard hundreds of "Well, I'll be damned!" responses *(delighted* "I'll be damneds") when I drew analogies like this one:

Suppose you're previewing a television commercial. Call it A. And B is a print advertisement you're about to place for the same product. What is there about A that you can apply to B?

Now, as you preview the TV spot (A), the producer says, "Wait till you hear the character in this voice-over—it's better than Orson Welles!" But then you listen and the voice sounds like the guy has loose dentures . . . and you can't understand a word. What do you say?

Of course! You say, "We'd better forget the character and get some clarity!"

You know a TV voice-over must come through so clearly that people will hear and understand it even when conversing with someone and not really watching the set. The voice has got to be heard—and easily understood—at that split-second decision point when viewers either say, "Wait a minute, I want to see this"—or they keep right on talking.

Now, for the headline of your print advertisement—B—you're using a typeface and setting that someone apparently thought had great character (clever, in other words). But that typeface is so difficult to read, no meaningful words reach out to grab readers' interest. Especially when readers are just idly turning pages, perhaps with their minds the proverbial million miles away.

Aren't the broadcast commercial and the print advertisement exactly alike in that their first job is to make people pause and, hopefully, stop?

And, in both cases, isn't that done by quickly making something of interest instantly clear to them, even when they're paying little or no attention? In the commercial with a truly easy-to-understand voice—and in the print advertisement with a truly easy-to-read typeface and setting?"

Now, here it comes: "Well, I'll be damned!"

To give you just one more example, I got the same, suddenly enlightened "I'll be damned" using another analogy. Clients readily agreed that, in a broadcast commercial, they knew they could not "get in every sales point" by having the voice-over speak way too fast—so fast no sales points were made clear.

"Then why," I asked, "do you expect, in this print advertisement, to get in every sales point by setting it in a typeface way too small—so small that people won't read *even one* of your sales points?"

Now let's generalize: You start toward good, effective typography when you see the relationships between verbal/visual and print/visual communications. Those relationships lead you to understand that the common operative word in both fields is communication.

In both fields, the key is to make things EASY for the viewer and reader.

While I've used analogies between TV commercials and print advertisement, what I really mean by "verbal/visual" is much broader than the world of advertising. I'm referring to everything you've learned since infancy about communication through verbal and visual means.

In other words, you start toward good, effective typographic communications when you apply to print what you now intellectually and intuitively know from your own life-long experience with all that's verbal and visual.

That's the *core* of what we must know and believe. But we have to build on that core, learning and applying more than the basics. In both broadcast and print, there are technical aspects—"fine points" that can greatly enhance our ability to communicate.

For example, in broadcast, those enhancements include background music, sound effects, and subtle techniques of cinematography. In print, some of the "fine points" are knowledge of reading patterns, styles of typefaces and specifications for settings that allow easy reading, and the unique opportunities (and dangers) of digitized typesetting.

That's why *Type & Layout* has such great value for anyone involved in print communications.

For as far back as I can remember, I have called typography "the voice of print." For I very early saw the relationship *between* voice and print. And I have worked by following the principle that what applies to one applies to the other. Anything inconsistent with that principle—or simply and obviously ego-indulgent, and thus not pragmatic—should not apply in either medium.

Working from that foundation, I made both my basic and "fine-point" decisions, with results that proved them right time after time. But, until Colin Wheildon came along, I had no "charts" with which to convince the literal-minded. That's why I respectfully, gratefully, and affectionately call him my "ally in the fight against bad typography."

Thank you, old friend and ally, Colin Wheildon, for proving—with unassailable research—the rules and guidelines by which I have worked and (immodestly I'll add) prospered. So too can the readers—and practitioners—of the truths in this book.

—Tony Antin

Tony Antin is the author of Great Print Advertising *(John Wiley & Sons, New York, 1993).*

The Research Program

MY FATHER WAS A DERBY, ENGLAND, master printer who held three truths to be self-evident:

» Rules and borders must meet like water.
» Serif text is much easier to comprehend than sans serif text.
» Editors and designers are the missing link between the ape world and man.

The first tenet is inarguable.

That it took me a quarter of a century as an editor and designer before I questioned the validity of the second tenet is testimony, in some measure, to the truth of the third.

Early in my career I had become aware that the rules of typography were largely ancient maxims, with very little, if any, empiricism to support them.

I was aware of research into legibility, which is to say the intrinsic characteristics that make one type easier to read than another.

But I was also aware that research into mere legibility did not provide the answers I wanted.

Figure 62

In a newspaper nameplate, Old English type like this is appropriate and expected. In the paper's news columns, it would take some getting used to.

Old English type

The title of a newspaper set in Old English text may well be legible, but what would happen if the entire news and advertising content were to be set in Old English? Would it be comprehensible to anyone, other than perhaps a scholar of early English calligraphy or printing?

In recent years I became a disciple of Edmund Arnold, formerly a professor of mass communications at Virginia Commonwealth University, Richmond, Virginia. Inspired by his common-sense teachings, but alarmed by the fact that even he depended on maxims rather than field research, I determined to subject some of those maxims to research.

This study is the result. It was conducted over a nine-year period, from 1982 to 1990.

THE PROGRAM EXAMINED SEVERAL ELEMENTS of typographic design. On two of them—the comprehensibility of serif type as opposed to sans serif in body matter, and the comprehensibility of lower case as opposed to capital letter headlines—there is, as I have indicated, some agreement, but very little observation of the agreement.

On three others—the use of color in headlines and in text, and the use of unjustified (ragged) setting, either left or right—there is either great disagreement or complete ignorance of the possible deleterious effects.

On a sixth element examined, whether italic body type is difficult or easy to comprehend, there appears to be a general, but ill-founded, agreement.

Texts on typography frequently allude to research into some of the elements to be examined, but, regrettably, discussion of this research is usually anecdotal rather than empirical.

In an attempt to test the reported findings of overseas research, the major part of this program was carried out in Sydney in 1982-86.

About the participants

A total of 224 people, drawn from 10 Sydney suburbs, completed the program.

The sample initially contained 300 people. As the years passed, some moved to other cities or towns, some died, some dropped out from sheer boredom, and some were committed to institutions for the chronically confused, as a result of being bombarded regularly with my experiment papers. All the result papers from those who dropped out were removed from the file so that the end results would not be weighted.

Initially, the sample had perfect balance of the sexes, with 150 men and 150 women. Fortunately, and fortuitously, this balance was nearly maintained, the final figures being 113 men and 111 women.

Responses from males and females showed no statistically significant variation.

Twenty of the readers were high school students. All the adults had completed four years of high school, and 178 (79 per cent) had reached matriculation level. Fifty-two (23 per cent) had acquired a university degree, or professional or trade qualification, and twelve (5 per cent) had acquired a higher degree. This indicates a higher than average education level, and obviously represents a bias in the sample. This was deliberate. The participants were those who would be expected to take an interest in current events, and consequently would be likely to be regular newspaper and magazine readers.

In fact, all except two indicated they were consistent readers of a range of newspapers and other publications. The other two, teenagers, said they read magazines regularly, but newspapers infrequently.

None of the readers was professionally involved in the printing or publishing industries.

The methodology

First I wrote two articles which were designed to have specific interest to members of the sample.

One article was about the plans for a local government authority to increase domestic rates, but to reduce the services to rate-payers. The article described the proposed increases and the reductions in services in detail. This article was geographically specific to sample members and was aimed squarely at their pocketbooks.

The second article was about plans to place parking meters in suburban streets, particularly outside private houses, and to enforce on-street parking laws by constant police surveillance. The article included police comments designed to inflame resident action groups and to provoke reactions from them.

I then devised a series of questions about major points in the articles, designed to discover whether the sample participants had read through the articles and digested the contents.

The 224 people were divided into two equal groups to provide a measure of control. This division enabled each group to read the same articles, but presented in alternative forms. They read the material, under supervision, and in a given time, then were asked a series of questions. They were not told the questions would attempt to determine the level of comprehension. The tests were repeated throughout the five years with the disbursement of papers reversed to minimize bias in responses.

Answers were rated thus: ten to seven correct, good; six to four, fair; three to none, poor.

Tests were supervised, and all were conducted in the readers' homes, under their normal reading conditions, in both daytime and evenings.

The questions were asked randomly, my view being that if design or other factors had a detrimental effect on comprehension, the point where comprehension declined could be deduced from the sequence of correct answers.

For example, if sample members consistently answered only three questions correctly, say questions 4, 6 and 10, and these referred to points in the first few paragraphs, it could be inferred that comprehension failed for some reason after the first few paragraphs.

If, however, using a different layout or other type or design element, more sample members answered more of the questions correctly, then it could be inferred that the design, or other type element, had had an effect on comprehension.

The fact that this consistently occurred, over a series of tests in the course of several years, led me to infer that typography was the prime culprit.

Following each formal test, I asked informal questions to gain anecdotal evidence. For example, from the informal questioning, sample members indicated they experienced eye fatigue and consequent loss of comprehension when the text was set in color, and that a colored headline distracted them from the black text which followed it.

Initially, the articles were set in two design styles: one in the format of Figure 9 (see page 36), the other in the format of Figure 10 (page 39). Half the sample were given the Figure 9 layout, which complies with Arnold's Gutenberg Diagram. Half received the Figure 10 layout, which does not.

Later, with another article, the sample groups were reversed. The first group was given the Figure 10 layout, and the second group was given the Figure 9 layout. This procedure was repeated several times over several years, and the sample groups were randomly selected each time.

After a few tests, it became apparent to me from the preliminary results that the Figure 10 layout (defying Arnold) was faulty. The results from using it were less than half as good as those from Figure 9 layouts. So, for future tests of other elements, Figure 10 was discarded and Figure 9 became the standard layout for testing serif versus sans serif and other factors.

I conducted all the research. I devised the page, performed the interviews, phrased and asked the questions, and collated the results. I did this to eliminate the possibility of the bias or distortion that might have occurred had I contracted others to do the work.

When the tests for a design element were completed, the results were collated first as a series of individual results to determine whether any statistically unacceptable deviations had occurred. None had.

The final averages were taken from the total calculation, not as averages of a series of averages.

My advisors

The catalyst for the methodology and procedures I used was the late Prof. Henry Mayer, Professor of Political Science at Sydney University and editor of the learned magazine *Media Information Australia*. When I mentioned to him that I was considering some research into elements of design and typography, he gave me several invaluable pieces of advice.

» Prof. Mayer's first piece of advice was to produce an acceptable methodology. There would be critics, he said, mainly among those who found the results disturbed their comfortable beds of subjective prejudice. They would attack on two fronts: *ad hominem*, which could be countered with ease, and on the method. If the method were faulty, the attack could not be countered.

» Moreover, Prof. Mayer said, if he found the methodology faulty he would personally crucify me, irrespective of whether the results confirmed or opposed his own prejudices about design.

» The next piece of advice was that I should attempt to eliminate all variables when testing a particular element. This advice led to a long sequence of experiments in which questionable design elements were progressively eliminated.

» Prof. Mayer also advised me to circulate the proposed methodology and results widely before publishing. If possible, he said, present them personally to a public forum, preferably to potential critics. This I did, using the Australian Creative Advertising Awards (the Caxtons), and the Australian Suburban Newspapers Association Congress, as forums.

I then sought the advice of Prof. Edmund Arnold, then Professor of Mass Communications at Virginia Commonwealth University, Richmond, Virginia, and Prof. Rolf Rehe, then of the Purdue Universities Consortium in Indianapolis, Indiana. Assisted by Prof. Mayer, I adapted Rolf Rehe's rate-of-work method to suit my experiments.

Prof. Mayer also advised me on sample selection.

I was advised on the conduct of the project by Dr. Simon Gadir, then Director of Research for the Newspaper Advertising Bureau of Australia. Dr. Gadir also advised me on such factors as statistical significance of results, and scales of confidence (the McLemar scale)—in other words, which numbers would stand up to scientific scrutiny, and which should be (and were) eliminated.

I also sought advice on method, calculation, analysis, and presentation of results from the following persons:

» Prof. David Sless, Executive Director of the Communications Research Institute of Australia;

» Professors Arnold, Rehe, and Mayer;

» David Ogilvy, who was a renowned researcher before he became the Pope of modern advertising;

» Bryce Courtenay, who, when he is not writing best-selling novels and screenplays (*The Power of One*), is Creative Director for the George Patterson Advertising Agency in Sydney;

» members of the academic staff of the University of Reading, which houses the British Government's forms design center;

» members of the academic staff of the Royal College of Arts in London; and

» Jim Thomson, then Head of Research for the National Roads and Motorists' Association Australia, one of the ten biggest motoring organizations in the world.

Comprehension—or readability?

Over the years of my research, David Ogilvy more than once raised the question whether I was measuring reading comprehension, or merely readability. I'm grateful for his persistence in moving me to confront this important—and difficult—question.

My difficulty stemmed from the fact that, in my *Shorter Oxford Dictionary*, readability has two distinct definitions:

1. *Capable of being read, legible*

2. *Capable of being read with pleasure or interest, usually of a literary work.*

This presented me with a dilemma. I was not testing legibility. That is a totally different discipline, and has been the subject of a considerable measure of scientific work. I wanted to know whether the nature of type or design affected the reader's ability to understand the text.

However, if I used the words readability and readable, they could be misconstrued as being analogous to legibility and legible.

So I settled on comprehensibility.

The essence is, as David Ogilvy suggests, that I was measuring the extent to which typography and design affected understanding. But to understand, one first has to read the message!

However, in Chapter 5, where I address the subject of headlines, I did not test comprehension, because the method did not permit it. There, I was testing whether headlines were easy to read or not. Those were the words used in the tests, and those were the words used by the sample members.

§ *APPENDIX 2*

Guide to Tables

§ *APPENDIX 3*

Guide to Illustrations

§

Glossary

A
ascending letters
Letters with a projection above the body, such as b, d, h, k, 1, *and* t.

Axis of Orientation
An imaginary line at the left of a column of type, to which the eye automatically returns after reading a line of type.

B

bastard measure

Text type in which the column width varies from the norm within an article. For example, bastard measure is used to accommodate a half column picture within the text.

black face or black letter

A type group which has straight thick and thin strokes meeting at acute angles, in imitation of priestly calligraphy. Old English and Fraktur are examples.

𝔒𝔩𝔡 𝔈𝔫𝔤𝔩𝔦𝔰𝔥 𝔱𝔶𝔭𝔢 𝔩𝔬𝔬𝔨𝔰 𝔩𝔦𝔨𝔢 𝔱𝔥𝔦𝔰.

body type

Small type set in blocks as text for continuous reading.

body text, body copy, body matter

The text of an article or advertisement, as opposed to the headline.

bold face

Type letter of normal form and size but with heavier strokes. Some typefaces have a black form, which is heavier than bold.

This is regular (or medium) type.

This is bold face in the same typeface.

This is extra black type.

C

capital

Larger letters, often called upper case letters, and used as initial letters or in headlines—hence the word capital. (Caput is Latin for head.)

circular line screen

A decorative screen in which a photograph or art image is contained in concentric circles, giving a telescopic or target effect.

coldset press

A printing press which uses no heat to dry the ink. Material printed coldset is more susceptible to smudging than if heat were applied during the printing process to dry the ink instantaneously.

comprehensibility

The intrinsic nature of the printed word which permits it to be read and understood, to the extent that the reader may take action on any message it contains.

comprehension

The ability to read text and understand it to such an extent as to be able, if appropriate, to take action on any messages it contains.

condensed

Type letters which have normal form and height, but which are narrower than normal. Many types are designed with a condensed form, and some have extra or ultra condensed forms. (See examples on next page.)

This is normal (or medium) type.

This is condensed type.

cursive
Typefaces that imitate handwriting.

This is a cursive typeface.

D

deck
A single line of a heading which has two or more lines.

descending letters
Letters with a projection below the body, such as g, j, p, q, and y.

display
Arrangement of typographical and design elements to make printed material attractive to the reader.

drop capital or drop initial
A *capital letter used to begin an article or section of an article, as in this paragraph. It may be two or more times as big as the body type, and may be inset into the beginning of the first two or three lines. When a drop initial is used, the first word of the text is usually set in capitals.*

E

editorial

In magazines and newspapers, text of news or feature articles as opposed to advertising matter.

eight on nine point or 8/9

A type size common in newspaper and magazine setting, which denotes a type that is eight points, or approximately 1/9 of an inch high, set on a body of nine points, or 9/72 of an inch high, thus providing an inbuilt interlinear space.

em, en

Widely-used measurements of type width equivalent to the widths of the letters m and n. Those widths vary from one typeface to another.

extended or expanded

The opposite of condensed. Type which has the same form and height as, but is wider than, the normal face.

This is regular (or medium) type.

This is extended type.

F

fix

A point at which display material being scanned attracts the reader's eyes, and which sends a subconscious message to the effect that this material looks interesting and may be worth reading.

G

gloss

The shine on paper often used for magazines or pamphlets. It may be chemically applied during paper manufacture, when it is known as coated paper, or it may be applied mechanically after paper manufacture by squeezing the paper between heavy steel rollers, when it is known as calendered paper. Coated paper is generally shinier and may provide more reading difficulty than calendered paper or matte paper.

greek

Stick-on type used by designers as a simulation of text to indicate positioning, usually when the actual text is not available. In desktop publishing programs, greek screen fonts simulate text in small point sizes. Paradoxically, greek type is usually Latin!

Gutenberg Diagram

Devised by Prof. Edmund Arnold, in honor of the 15th-century German inventor of movable type, this diagram shows how a reader approaches and reads a page of printed material. (See Figure 8, page 34.)

high chroma

Chroma is the characteristic which indicates the brightness of an ink color. Examples of high chroma are hot red, lime green, yellow, or cyan.

H

horizontal line screen

A decorative screen in which the photograph or art image is contained in horizontal lines, giving the effect of looking at the picture through venetian blinds.

hot metal

All metallic printing material, including type and illustration blocks, as opposed to photographic or computer-created material.

humanist

Sans serif typefaces based on the proportions of inscriptional roman lettering. Humanist faces, such as Optima, Pascal, and Gill Sans, have some variation between thick and thin strokes, which sans serif faces generally lack.

This typeface is a variant of Optima, a humanist face.

I

italic

Roman type style that slants to the right, as in this phrase. The term italic should be reserved for Roman faces; other faces that slant to the right are called oblique. See also roman.

J

jobbing or job printing

The commercial printing of leaflets, pamphlets, mailers, or inserts for magazines or newspapers.

jump

Continuation of an article on a later page or pages. This occurs occasionally in newspapers, but most frequently in magazines, where readers often are subjected to several pages at the rear which contain the spillage from articles displayed earlier in the magazine.

justified type

Type set so that both margins are straight.

K

kerned type

Type in which the natural inter-letter space is electronically reduced.

This type is set natural, without kerning.

This type has been kerned one-tenth of an em.

L

light face

Type letter of normal form and size, but with reduced stroke width.

This is normal (or medium) type.

This is the light variation on the same typeface.

light roman

A roman serif face with normal form and size, vertical, but with a reduced stroke width.

low chroma

Ink colors that lack brightness. Examples are olive green, gray, and black.

lower case

Little letters, such as are used in text. The term comes from the early period of hand-set and metal or wooden type: the compositor had two cases of type–the lower case had the little letters and the upper case the capitals.

M

matte

Dull or unglazed finish on paper. Most newsprint and book papers are matte. Magazine papers generally are glossy.

medium face

The standard intensity for most type faces. This book is set largely in Goudy OldStyle, medium.

mezzo screen

A decorative screen in which the image is contained in large irregular dots, producing a crayon or pastel effect.

minus spacing

The measure of electronically kerned type, where inter-letter space is reduced from the natural setting.

This type is set natural.

Kerning can make letters overlap.

modern

Roman typefaces with severe contrast between thick and thin strokes and horizontal thin serifs, often without brackets linking them to the vertical or horizontal strokes. The name modern is a misnomer, referring as it does to a type style developed at the end of the 18th century. The standard name for modern is now Didone.

This is Bernhard Modern, a modern typeface.

multi-deck heading

Headline that has several lines, usually more than three.

N

natural type or set natural

Type set in its natural form, without artificial space reduction or expansion.

O

oblique

Only roman types that lean to the right are italic. All others are called oblique. Type that leans to the left is usually called backslant. I prefer to use the term "deformed."

old face

Roman faces in which the serifs are bracketed to the vertical or horizontal strokes, and with minimal variation in thickness between horizontals and verticals.

This is a typeface of the "old face" family.

This is a modern typeface, with unbracketed serifs.

P

photocomposition

Type set by photographic means, as opposed to mechanical (hot metal) means.

photomechanical transfer

These used to be known as PMTs, until the initials became more widely known to denote a medical condition. A photomechanical transfer is a black and white photographic reproduction of a page of type and display images. They are sometimes known as bromide proofs. (A common trade name is Velox.)

pica

A printer's unit of measurement, equal to 12 points. Six picas are about equal to one inch, or 72 points. Pica was formerly used to denote 12 point type. The type on these lines is 24 picas wide (four inches). See also point.

PMS

PMS is the Pantone Matching System, an internationally recognized system of denoting printing colors. The system provides accurate proportions of inks required to make a specific color, which is then given a PMS number. For example, PMS 259 is a deep purple and PMS 286 is French blue. PMS colors are generally used on sheet-fed presses, which can print more than four colors on a single sheet of paper in one pass.

point

The basic unit of measurement in printing, approximately 1/72 of an inch. Pica therefore is about one sixth of an inch. Seventy-two point type is about one inch high. (See examples on next page.)

This is 6 point type.

This is 18 point type.

54 point

Primary Optical Area

In Edmund Arnold's Gutenberg Diagram, the Primary Optical Area (POA) is the point at which the reader's eyes enter, or are attracted into, a page. It is, or should be, the top left corner of a page, or of a type area.

process colors

High speed multi-impression printing uses three ink colors (plus black), which are called the process colors. They are cyan (blue), yellow (lemon), and magenta (red). Each color is printed on one plate, the impression from which is superimposed on the other three to give the effect of full-color printing. Process colors can be used on any press, but are the standard form for web presses, which generally have the capacity to print four colors only on continuous reeled paper.

R

ragged left

A style of type setting in which the left margin is uneven. This style is sometimes used in advertising material.

ragged right

A style of type setting in which the right margin is uneven. It was developed to eliminate the need, in book setting, for uneven inter-word spacing or hyphens. However, there is no research-based justification to consider either a problem for the reader.

readable, readability, reading

Where these terms are used, the secondary definition (in the Shorter Oxford Dictionary) *is implied:* capable of being read with pleasure or interest, usually of a literary work; agreeable or attractive in style. *What is not implied is the primary definition, which makes* readable *synonymous with* legible.

reverse

Type set white on black, or on a dark colored background.

roman

Vertical type style with serifs and variation of thickness in strokes, including curved strokes.

This is a roman face.

S

sans serif

Type style without serifs, and usually with minimal or no variation in thickness of strokes. The standard name for sans serif, which has many variations, is Lineale.

This is a sans serif typeface.

serif

The small tick-like stroke at the end of the main stroke of a letter. The origin of the word is obscure, but may be from the Dutch word schreef, a stroke. Serifs were used in roman inscriptional writing as a means of finishing off the lapidary work.

Some serifs are straight, others appear sculptured.

Some serifs are straight, others appear sculptured.

shade

A color value achieved by adding black to a color (see tint).

spot color

A single color used as a display feature.

T

Terminal Anchor

A device used to indicate to the reader that the article has ended.

tint
A color value achieved by adding white to a color (see shade).

U
unjustified text
Text with irregular edges at both left and right margins.

upper case
Big or capital letters (see lower case).

W
widow
Two schools of thought offer varying definitions of a widow, although both agree that the main criterion is a short line–less than half the full measure. One school says a widow appears at the foot of the column; the other says that a widow is the first line of the next column. The author has grown up with the latter definition, and is unshakable.

X

x-height

The height in a typeface of the letter x, which is also the height of all median letters (those without ascending or descending strokes). The height of type is measured from the top of the ascender to the foot of the descender. The greater the x-height of the median letters (such as x), the greater the perceived height of the type and its inherent legibility–and the greater the certainty of deciphering (the criterion for comprehension).

A typeface with a large x-height.

A typeface with a small x-height.

§

Recommended Reading

Antin, Tony, *Great Print Advertising*, John Wiley & Sons (New York), 1993

Arnold, Edmund C., *Arnold's Ancient Axioms: Typography for Publications Editors*, Ragan Report Press (Chicago), 1978

————, *Designing the Total Newspaper*, Harper and Row (New York), 1981

Evans, Harold, *Newspaper Design*, Holt, Rinehart & Winston (Orlando, Florida), 1973

McLean, Ruari, *The Thames and Hudson Manual of Typography*, Thames and Hudson (London), 1980, 1992

Moran, James, *Stanley Morison*, Lund Humphries, 1971

Morison, Stanley, *First Principles of Typography*, Cambridge University Press, 1936

———, *The Art of Printing*, Humphrey Milford, 1938

———, *The Typographic Arts, Past, Present and Future*, James Thin, 1944

Ogilvy, David, *Confessions of an Advertising Man*, Atheneum (New York), 1963

———, *Ogilvy on Advertising*, Crown Publishers (New York), 1983

Rehe, Rolf, *Typography: How to Make it Most Legible*, Design Research International, 1983

———, *Typography and Design for Newspapers*, Design Research International, 1985

Tinker, Miles A., *Legibility of Print*, Iowa State University Press, 1963

§

Index

A

B

bold face   84, 99, 102

brightness   86, 93

British Medical Council   56

broadcast   179 - 180

C

D

F

G

H

I

J

K

L

lower case   *31, 33, 62 - 68, 73 - 75, 114, 127, 185*

M

magazines   *8 - 9, 12 - 13, 19 - 20, 28 - 30, 43 - 46, 48, 50, 53, 55 - 56, 58, 61, 63, 79, 109 - 110, 115, 117, 122, 124, 129 - 130, 136, 169, 191*

magenta   *79 - 80, 83*

magnet   *40, 78, 80*

mailings   *14*

marketing   *12, 88, 94, 96, 101 (see also direct marketer)*

matte   *85*

maxims   *33, 184 - 185*

Mayer, Henry   *190 - 192*

McKinnon, Harvey   *13 - 14*

McLemar scale   *192*

Media Information Australia   *191*

medium intensity color   *85, 87, 99 (see also color, high intensity color, low intensity color)*

message   *10, 22 - 24, 50, 58, 69, 78, 82, 101 - 102, 113, 119, 133 - 134, 138, 140, 145, 163, 194*

methodology   *35, 187 - 191*

mezzotype   *123*

minus spacing   *68*

modern   *62, 66 - 67, 73*

monotonal strokes 55

Morison, Stanley 27 - 28, 30

multi-deck heading 71, 124, 127 *(see also decks, headlines)*

N

narrow measure 125, 127

National Roads and Motorists' Association Australia 193

natural 48, 64, 69, 72, 74, 111, 113 - 114, 119, 123, 144
    (see also set natural)

New South Wales 139

newspaper 30, 32, 43, 53, 55, 60 - 62, 79, 84, 115, 123,
    129 - 130, 144, 184 - 185

Newspaper Advertising Bureau of Australia 192

O

oblique 31 *(see also italic)*

Ogilvy, David 8, 61, 97, 117, 130, 136, 138, 192 - 194

Old English 75, 184 - 185

old face 62

optical effect 56

optical magnet 38 *(see also eye, eye movement)*

optically-designed 55

Optima   55 - 56, 66 - 68

ornamented typeface   66

P

Pantone Matching System (PMS)   84 (see also color)

paper   10, 77, 84 - 86, 88

periods   12, 115 - 117, 119 - 120, 159, 163, 165, 167

photo-composition   69

photographs   138

photomechanical transfer   72

phototypesetter   72

physiology of reading   19, 32, 48, 63, 147, 151

placement   37, 49 (see also layout)

points   140 - 145

Primary Optical Area (POA)   33 - 34, 40, 48 (see also Gutenberg Diagram)

print communications   178 - 181

printer   10, 183

process blue   79, 84, 86, 88

process color   79, 81, 149 (see also color, process blue)

Purdue Universities Consortium   192

R

ragged left   108 - 110, 163, 167, 171 (see also justified margins, ragged right)

ragged right   12, 107 - 110, 163, 172 (see also justified margins, ragged left)

rate-of-work method   192

readability   193-194

reading gravity   33, 36, 38 - 48, 50, 149 (see also Gutenberg Diagram)

reading patterns   181 (see also eye movement)

reading rhythm   28, 33, 37 - 38, 40, 43, 108, 149

recall   59, 138

Rehe, Rolf   192

research   8, 12 - 13, 17, 31, 33, 35, 40 - 41, 44, 48, 56, 62, 67, 78, 82 - 84, 110, 113, 129 - 130, 135 - 136, 138 - 140, 147, 181, 183   187, 189, 191, 193

reverse   8, 84, 97, 119, 167

reversed body type   12, 98, 121

roman type   23, 31, 43 - 44, 62, 66 - 67, 72 - 73, 75, 99, 103 - 105, 109

Royal College of Arts   193

rules   149, 177, 181, 183

S

T

W

warm red   84, 86 - 87
Warwick, Mal   16, 17
Welles, Orson   178
Wheildon, Colin   8, 12 - 15, 181
wide measure   121, 125 - 127
widows   121, 125

X

x-height   41, 104

§

About the Author

COLIN WHEILDON was born in Warwickshire, England in 1936, the son of a printer, and migrated to Australia with his parents in 1950. He left school in 1954 to become a cub reporter on the *Mackay Daily Mercury*, a newspaper in tropical Queensland.

Colin qualified as a full-fledged journalist after only two years as a cadet, and by his 21st birthday was editor of the *Western Star* newspaper in Roma, a cattle town in western Queensland.

In 1958 he became an editor of *The Sydney Daily Telegraph*, one of Australia's major newspapers, now part of the Murdoch group. He later became News Editor of *TV Times*, then Australia's biggest television magazine.

Colin took a break from print in the 1970s to become, among other things, radio and television publicity chief for Australia's national broadcaster, the ABC. He returned to print in 1979 when he joined the National Roads and Motorists' Association magazine, *The Open Road*, which he converted from a tabloid newspaper to a full-color litho magazine.

In 1982 he began the research which has culminated in this book, and which has become an international benchmark study on the effects of typographic elements on the reader.

During his term as Managing Editor of *The Open Road* from 1988 to 1993, the magazine became Australia's biggest circulation publication. By applying the results of his research, he was able to increase the magazine's readership by nearly 40 per cent, from 1.6 million to nearly 2.3 million.

Colin has been visiting lecturer at the University of Western Sydney in Australia, design consultant to the Pacific Islands News Association, and most recently an honorary tutor in early literacy for children with specific learning difficulties.

His research recently was adopted by the New South Wales State Government, and influences design standards for all new state legislation aimed at improving comprehension in Australia.

He now lives with his wife, Lynn, in the lakeside village of Mannering Park, in the state of New South Wales, where they operate a typography and design consultancy.

§

About the Typography in This Book

TYPE & LAYOUT is largely a product of amateur desktop publishing. Discerning typographers and designers may well have concluded as much long before now.

We scanned the text of the booklet on which this book is based, *Communicating–Or Just Making Pretty Shapes?* (Third Australian Edition). Then I edited the text, using WordPerfect for Windows 6.0a running on a garden-variety 66 megahertz, IBM-compatible i486 PC. Using Corel Ventura 4.2, I then typeset and formatted the entire book (except for the cover). To produce camera-ready artwork, I printed the text on high-resolution laser paper at 1200 dots per inch on an enhanced Hewlett-Packard LaserJet 4M.

The text of this book is a TrueType version of Goudy OldStyle from Ares Software Corp., set 12.5 points on a 14 point body. Chapter headings, titles, and subheads are in Bitstream's Goudy Handtooled.

The editor will cheerfully receive all comments, negative or positive, about this book's typography and design. While I benefitted hugely from the advice of several skilled professional typographers and designers, including the author, I hold them all blameless. The flaws in this book are of my doing. Others, especially Colin Wheildon, have taught me a great deal, but I've still got a lot to learn.

By contrast, however, the cover art was professionally prepared by Marianne Wyss. She worked her magic on an Apple Macintosh IIcx using PageMaker 5.0.

—M.W.

§

"Raise more money for your favorite charity"

IF YOU WORK FOR A NONPROFIT ORGANIZATION or serve on a charity's board, you know how tough it is to raise the funds your organization needs. Now there's a book that can help you meet that challenge—and it's fun to read!

In *How to Write Successful Fundraising Letters*, fundraising guru Mal Warwick has crammed into one book every bit of insight he could muster from fifteen years raising money by mail. (More than $100,000,000 at last count!)

A leading trade publication for professional fundraisers called *How to Write Successful Fundraising Letters* "the definitive guide to writing fundraising letters—sure to become the standard against which others are measured. Practical, written with extreme clarity, enjoyable to read (thanks to the author's engaging style), and, most important of all, presents a storehouse of sound and usable concepts, principles, and techniques."

In this remarkable book by the noted fundraising consultant, columnist, and lecturer, you'll learn "The Cardinal Rules of Writing Fundraising Letters" . . . "What Donors Really Think About Fundraising Letters" . . . and "Twenty-Three Reasons People Respond to Fundraising Appeals."

The *Baltimore Sun* wrote, "This gem of a book is a no-nonsense guide to everything you want to know about direct mail fund-raising. Unlike far too many books of this ilk on the market today, this one is a nuts and bolts, soup to nuts exploration of the topic, written by one of the masters of direct mail fundraising."

How to Write Successful Fundraising Letters is a handsome hardback book of 251 large (8-1/2 x 11") pages, and it's jam-packed with real-world examples, illustrations, and case studies that reflect the latest research findings about how to secure gifts from today's donors. Yet it's only $39.95 (plus $4.00 S&H)! You'll use this book every time you write a fundraising letter. 3rd Printing.

» *To order with MasterCard or Visa, call toll-free (800)-217-7377, Dept. T. Or write Strathmoor Press, Inc., 2550 Ninth Street, Suite 1040, Berkeley, CA 94710-2516. When ordering, please mention item #S1005.*

"The best introduction to raising money by mail!"

Both experts and beginners can learn from Mal Warwick's comprehensive introduction to *Raising Money by Mail: Strategies for Growth and Financial Stability.*

Originally published in 1990 under the title *Revolution in the Mailbox* and sold at $65.00, this book was quickly acclaimed as the standard in its field. Now revised and updated, this classic text is profusely illustrated, set in large, readable type, and written in an easy, down-to-earth style. Here's the way to *understand* the obscure world of raising money by mail!

Mary Herman, then Executive Director of the Nonprofit Mailers Federation, called *Revolution in the Mailbox* "a must read for anyone new to direct mail fundraising—and a great reference for the practitioner who has been around the field. The examples are great! You can tell these are based on real organizations, not pie-in-the-sky theories."

Nonprofits and fundraising agencies use this book to train staff members. Charities distribute copies to board members. Now available for $19.95 (plus $4.00 S&H) per copy. (Discounts available on quantity purchases.) Call (510) 843-8888 for details. Softcover, 128 pages (8-1/2 x 11").

» *To order with MasterCard or Visa, call toll-free (800)-217-7377, Dept. T. Or write Strathmoor Press, Inc., 2550 Ninth Street, Suite 1040, Berkeley, CA 94710-2516. When ordering, please mention item #S1006.*

"The very best working ... volumes available on the use of graphics in books and publications."

That's how Publisher's Weekly describes the books of Jan White, former Time Magazine Art Director and author of *Color for Impact: How color can get your message across– or get in the way.*

Every designer knows that color grabs attention and raises a viewer's perception of quality. But–if used properly–it also can initiate action, improve recall, sell more, and boost productivity! This groundbreaking title shows how to use color to get noticed and have the strongest impact possible. White not only illustrates his proven rules, but also explains why they work.

Learn when and how to use different colors, the secrets of their symbolism and psychological implications, and which gradients and combinations are most effective in different media. A wealth of examples–newsletters, flyers, posters, inter-office memos, policy covers, and more– show you why Jan White's Ten Commandments of color must be followed.

Any writer, designer, or desktop publisher will find this fast-reading classic hard to put down and easy to use!

» *To order with MasterCard or Visa, call toll-free (800)217-7377, Dept. T. Or write Strathmoor Press, Inc., 2550 Ninth Street, Suite 1040, Berkeley, CA 94710-2516.*

For a free catalog,
or for additional copies of this book,
contact the publisher:

Strathmoor Press, Inc.
2550 Ninth Street, Suite 1040
Berkeley, California 94710-2516
Toll-free credit-card orders: (800) 217-7377
For more information, call (510) 843-8888
Fax (510) 843-0142
E-mail info@strathmoor.com

STRATHMOOR
PRESS